Jessica Rees was born at Head Master's House, Eton College, on 19 April 1963. Her grandfather Sir Robert Birley was then head master and her father a house master at Eton. At the age of four she went profoundly deaf as a result of meningitis, becoming totally deaf thirteen years later following a hit-and-run accident. In 1982 she became the first totally deaf student at Oxford University, where she is reading English.

JESSICA REES

Sing a Song of Silence

A Deaf Girl's Odyssey

Futura
Macdonald & Co
London & Sydney

A Futura Book

First published in Great Britain in 1983
by The Kensal Press

This Futura edition published in 1984

ISBN 0 7088 2567 2

Printed in Great Britain by Collins.

Futura Publications
A Division of
Macdonald & Co (Publishers) Ltd
Maxwell House
74 Worship Street
London EC2A 2EN
A BPCC plc Company

Contents

Table of Events

1963 19th April	Jessica's birth
1965	Family left Eton, moved to Northwood
1967	Deafened by meningitis
1971 September	Entered St Helen's School
1973 August	Family left Northwood, moved to Godalming
1973 September	Entered St Mary's School, Shackleford
1974 September	Entered Tormead School, Guildford
1975 19th August	Entered Mary Hare Grammar School for the Deaf
1978 10th December	Jessica's mother dies
1979 August	Outward Bound Course R 204 in Wales
1980 June	Left Mary Hare School
1980 August	Victim of hit-and-run accident
1980 10th September	Joined the Sixth Form at Charterhouse
1981 10th December	Interviewed at Balliol College, Oxford on third anniversary of mother's death
1982 October	Joined Balliol College, Oxford

Acknowledgements.

In spite of not wanting to embarrass anyone concerned by making flowery, theoretical speeches about them, I would, nevertheless, like to show my appreciation of the help given me by those who made a significant contribution to my work.

I would first of all like to thank David Lincoln for implanting the idea of a book in my mind and persuading me that I could indeed do it. I am also grateful to Ann and Ezra Rachlin who gave me so much help and encouragement this last year, and enabled me weather the bad patches as well as enjoy the good ones. I would too like to mention Dr. Margaret Bickerton of the Nuffield Hearing and Speech Centre who has been a constant giver of support ever since I first became deaf. Without her help in those early years, it is unlikely that I would ever even have possessed the ability to write this book.

Special thanks are due to my Grandmother – it was in the peace and quiet of her Somerset house that much of this was written, and to Juliet Gowan, a great friend of my mother, for giving me her very kind permission to include two of her poems in this book. I am indebted to Cameron Robert McCracken for all the invaluable advice he has given me, and to my publishing company – the Kensal Press for the infinite amount of trouble they have taken.

Last but not least I must not forget to thank my friends at Balliol, Marc, Wayne, Lorraine and Penny who nagged me no end into "getting on with it!" Without their (frequent) pestering this book might still be a half forgotten manuscript lying at the bottom of a dusty drawer.

J. Rees.

This book is dedicated to the memory of my mother,
Julia Rees, who died in 1978 after a long illness.
Without her, this would never have been written.
I owe it all to her.

Ache

I thought you were gone for good and I did not care.
  Then I remembered, suddenly, unexpectedly,
Reading an isolated poem, how you had talked
So warmly about Emily Dickinson. Listening, I was aware
Of the huge rough hole you had left, and that it hasn't
    healed.

My eyes went up from the page to the grey window
And the noise of drills in the street, enquiring their meaning;
And I couldn't help noticing – I didn't mean to,
But I couldn't help noticing, that in this room
  There are too many empty chairs,
And only one person – a stranger – about whom
  I do not know, or care.

However I shovel to fill up the hole with words,
  The edges are jagged and bare,
And the drilling pain, the shudder is still there.

– Juliet Gowan

PROLOGUE

I'm writing this in the hope of telling people all over the world something about deaf people and, in particular, about myself. But I mustn't let it become a fantasy about the way I'd like to be. And, I must warn you, it won't be the sort of sad story which some people like, about a poor little girl with a handicap. There are plenty of 'weepies' on the station bookstalls already.

I'm not ashamed to be deaf – why should I be? My disability isn't my fault. Nor does it make me feel abnormal. Some people don't believe that the deaf can live normally but, as I hope to show, we can. It's the way others treat us that is abnormal.

I am the same as you in that I can see, learn and reason things out like you. I feel hungry and thirsty like you. I have blood, a name, needs and wishes like you. I am different in that my ears don't work like yours and I am not able to listen, or perceive sounds, in the same way as you. Yet is there anyone in this world who isn't *different* in some way and, by other people's standards, *defective* in some way? We all suffer from some sort of disorder – deafness just seems to be one which it is easy to generalise about.

I am a person in my own right, an individual just as you are. I would like to be respected and trusted. I would like to be *considered*, but don't want more consideration than anybody else. Do other normal nineteen-year-old girls have to assert so many apparently obvious things? Do I really need to myself? I'm afraid I think I do: a lot of other deaf people do, as well. I hope I can show you why.

CHAPTER ONE

I Spy Death

My recollections of hospital life are somewhat patchy but I can clearly recall that I woke up feeling as if my head was going to explode and my neck felt as if it were enclosed in hard steel calipers. I could not see properly: all I could make of my surroundings were bright white lights and a blur of figures in white coats which kept coming and going. Cool hands would often touch my forehead and stroke my cheek – my mother's familiar perfume lingered constantly in the air. Yet I felt helpless. I could not reach out to them or answer their murmuring voices, it was as if some force was preventing me from doing so. I lay there feeling limp and semi-paralysed, unable to respond, angrily urging my unco-operative limbs to move. I felt as if my arms were bound tightly to my chest but I knew they were lying alongside my body, just dangling and useless. They did not feel part of me but numb and lifeless with tubes and drips entering and leaving them all over the place.

Fortunately this condition did not last long and eventually I began to be able to feel my arms and legs again. They began to move slightly when I willed them to. My neck became increasingly moveable and the headache subsided. My eyes began to focus more and more accurately on near and distant objects. The doctor who visited me twice daily looked more and more 'smiley' every day. It dawned on me that whatever I'd been through, however awful it had been, it was almost over.

My parents visited me constantly throughout and one day my mother said, 'Jessica, it's time you were out of bed on your feet again. Why don't you just take a little walk to the table where the other children have lunch, eat lunch there, and walk back?' Nervously they all waited. Would I be able to walk again? Had my legs been damaged in any way at all after the semi-paralysis had worn off? I swung my legs over to one side of the bed and couldn't believe what I saw! My legs were like matchsticks. It suddenly struck me as absurd and I started to laugh. One by one my Mum, the doctor and the nurse joined in until eventually ten other children in the ward left the lunch table to come and see what was happening. We ended up having a 'skinny legs' contest which I won outright amid gales of laughter and cheers of mirth accompanied by enthusiastic clapping.

After the nurses had shooed the children away I took hold of the doctor's supporting hands as he bent in front of me and slowly raised myself until my legs were supporting my weight. It was a weird feeling as I had not used my legs for nearly two weeks since the start of my illness at home. I felt light-headed and dizzy. I saw a worried, anxious expression on my mother's face which vanished immediately she caught my eye and turned into a reassuring smile. 'Go on,' she said, 'walk.'

I put one foot in front of the other. This was harder than it had ever been before. I could not co-ordinate the movements of my legs and, despite my efforts, much of my leg movements consisted of involuntary jerks and twitches as I struggled to put my foot down firmly on the ground. My knees felt as if they were just about to give way and wobble over, and I slowly became aware of something else as well. There was a deadly hush all over the ward. Action had come to a standstill and everybody was staring in my direction. Even the children at the lunch table had stopped their soup spoons in midstream to their open mouths and were gazing intently at me with wide-eyed innocence. One little boy even had his fingers crossed and I noticed a look of urgency on the doctor's face which had not been there before. I persevered until I was halfway to the table and then I suddenly collapsed unable to keep up the effort much longer. Then the tense atmosphere relaxed, the doctor scooped me up into his arms smiling broadly, the children were hitting the table with their soup spoons as a means of applause, soup splashed everywhere, much to the canteen servers' horror – and my mother was laughing as she reached out for me. I was going to be all right.

They sat me at the lunch table and I can't remember much of what happened after that except that the green pea soup was nauseating and I baulked at the smell before I even tasted it as they raised the spoon to my mouth. I caught my mother's eye and gave her a look of utter disgust which made her have a giggling fit. In order to get away from a potentially embarrassing situation my mother had to pick me up and put me back to bed feeding me tangerine segments with her back turned to the canteen servers as she struggled to regain control of herself.

Day by day my legs grew stronger and less and less wobbly. Soon I was able to walk a few paces by myself without any assistance. At length, I could be left alone on the loo without constant supervision to make sure I did not fall off. This was indeed a great achievement.

Yet life was not all roses for I still had bad days when my head hurt or my back ached and my legs refused to do what I wanted them to do. On those days I could be extremely difficult and stubborn, even to the point of being unco-operative with the doctors and nurses. It was on one such day that my mother took rather a long time to fetch some tangerines from the shops for me. By the time she returned I was in a blind rage and upon receiving the tangerines I burst open the brown paper bag and threw them all at her one by one. She seemed rather startled but without saying anything she picked them all up and placed them in the fruit bowl by my bed. Maddened by her silence I then picked up the water jug and deliberately poured three pints of Robinsons lemon barley water all over the floor. This time she gave me an exasperated look and drew her index finger across her throat at the nurse on duty who fetched a cleaning lady and the mess was cleared up in less than a minute, down to the last detail of my water jug being refilled. This very passivity roused me even further and this time I snatched up a wax crayon and began scribbling frantically on my bedclothes with it. The effect was instantaneous. A flicker of life darted into my mother's eye and she reached for my hand and gave me a resounding smack across my knuckles. I screamed in anger and she put her hand across my mouth to try and shut me up. I bit her hand and before long was on the receiving end of a series of sharp smacks across the tops of my still matchstick-like legs. It was at that point that I decided to call a truce and to begin negotiating peace terms.

Until a couple of months before I'd had to go into hospital, our family had a nanny, called Katherine, for some years. She had left us to train as a nurse and by sheer coincidence was training at the very hospital I was in. Like many children of my age, I refused to drink up my milk. The sessions when milk was served became open warfare between the nurses and myself. They would give it to me and I would refuse point-blank to drink it. They would then themselves raise the cup to my lips and I would knock it out of their hands. If I was lucky I usually managed to soak the bedclothes as well thus scoring more points against them since they would then have the additional task of changing my sheets. In short I rebelled in every way I could against 'drinking up my milk like a good little girl'. The periods in between, when no milk was served, were regarded as one would a cease-fire.

Then one day the tide turned against me as Katherine by some stroke of fate was transferred to my ward as part of her training programme. She arrived in the ward just as another 'milk drinking session' was about to commence and was immediately awarded the unenviable task of giving me my milk. It is not known to this day why the ward sister gave her that job. Maybe it was because all the other nurses were fed up with it since it usually meant a change of uniform afterwards, or maybe it was in order to test Katherine out – to see how she would react to my obnoxiousness. With a smile Katherine picked up my glass of milk and strode over to my bed aware that the other nurses were waiting cautiously to see what would happen. As she reached my bed Katherine bent over and whispered to me, 'Now drink your milk'. I baulked and she went on, 'I'll tell your daddy of you and he'll give you such a big smack that you won't be able to sit down for a whole week.' Stunned, I obediently took the glass from her and drained it angelically to the last drop, and Katherine grinned, took the glass from me, gave me a kiss and a wink and calmly walked back over to where the nurses were watching, aghast, with disbelieving expressions on their faces which said, 'How on earth did you manage that?' to which Katherine replied with a modest smile. I seldom refused to drink my milk after that.

I remember waking up one morning to find a newcomer, a boy about my age, asleep in a bed nearby me. He had blond curly hair and really long eyelashes which rested on his cheek as he slept. My mother looked at him but did not say anything – just looked serious and somewhat sad as she shuffled a pack of cards and began to play snap with me. About half an hour later the little boy's parents came in and sat hand in hand by his bed. They too looked very sad. I asked my mother why they didn't wake the little boy up since his parents had come all the way to visit him. Surely, I argued, isn't it rude to fall asleep in front of one's guests? My mother just motioned me to be quiet and said in a low voice that the boy was very ill and would not wake up. At this point the boy's mother addressed my mother and my Mum stopped playing snap with me and went over to the other side of my bed and spoke to them. They sat talking for what seemed like hours and it was only the tone in which they were conducting their conversation which prevented me from continually tugging impatiently at my mother's sleeve. I kept hearing my name mentioned and the word 'coma', and names of evil-sounding compounds. From time to time they made comparisons between him and me and my mother kept saying, 'Well, we've been so lucky over Jessica.' After which the parents would smile vaguely at me. Eventually the conversation came to an end and the parents left the ward. My mother came back over to my bed looking very solemn. She told me that the little boy had the same illness as I had had. 'Was he as ill as I was?' I queried (I was rather proud of the fact that I had nearly died). My mother said that, no, he was not as ill as I had been, but that he was younger than I, which made matters worse. 'Surely he'll get better then?' I asked, but my mother just shrugged her shoulders and carried on dealing out the cards for one last game before she had to go.

That afternoon the boy regained consciousness briefly and put his hands up to his head and screamed with pain. His parents were there trying to calm him down but without much success. Doctors and nurses kept coming and going from his bed which had curtains drawn all around. It was early evening before the curtains were pulled back. The rest of us children peered forward inquisitively 'to see if there was any blood' and were somewhat disconcerted to find him peacefully fast asleep while his parents sat motionless holding his hands.

That night while I was asleep I was woken up by the sound of a trolley. The light was on at the little boy's bedside with the curtains drawn around it and shadowy figures moving about within. I just grumbled mildly and stuck my head under the pillow. Occasions like this were not at all rare in our ward. Some time later, the light went off again, the curtains were drawn back and peace reigned once more.

It was broad daylight when I woke up. I blinked at the strong sunlight, yawned, and stretched myself before sitting up. I realised something was not quite right. I glanced around and saw my mother talking to the little boy's parents in the far corner of the ward. I waved to her and then turned to see how the little boy was. His bed was empty. He had died in the night.

My thoughts were vague and confused. I was too small to know or understand much about the seriousness of meningitis and its dangers, and once the initial shock was over, the rest of the children recovered and our ordinary busy life went on as usual – we forgot to think about the little boy with curly blond hair who had been with us for such a short time. Yet something must have stayed in my memory because the horror had bitten really deep. I think I was aware that it might have happened to me.

A few days later, my friendly doctor came over to my bed beaming. For a joke, as he approached my bed, he went through the motions of a boxer preparing to tackle his opponent.

'Well, well, well,' he said in that frightful hearty voice some doctors will choose to adopt. 'Come with me and we'll do a few tests on you to make sure you are well and truly fit again.' I immediately baulked stubbornly. I hated tests. He did not cease to smile, however. He just said, 'And if you're good, we might let you go home this afternoon.' Quick as a flash my frown vanished and I allowed him to take my hand and lead me out of the ward while I smiled and waved like a famous celebrity to everyone else with my free hand. The tests that followed were done very quickly, unusually co-operative as I was. When they were all over the doctor led me back to the ward, giving me a pick-a-back along the last few corridors or so, and told the nurses to take the stitches out of my ankle where a drip feed had entered during the more serious phase of my illness. That was horrible! I remember lying on the bed holding a nurse's hand very tightly whilst bathed in a sweat. Another nurse was steadying my leg while the stitches were slowly cut away one by one. All I could think was: 'Oh please God make them hurry up and I promise I'll never refuse to drink my milk again.' Every time they cut a stitch, the nurse said, 'One more to go.'

The doctor came back and took me on his knee.

'You are completely healthy now, young lady, so let's keep it that way, shall we? Take your tablets when you are told to and rest in the afternoons and be sure to go to bed when Mummy says so. And I don't want any fuss when you have your injections. But above all, Jessica,' he said, a broad grin spread over his face, 'be sure to drink your milk.' My mother groaned.

He said goodbye and left. As soon as he was out of the door my mother and I began packing at top speed in case he came back with a second opinion.

When I left hospital that afternoon I was completely better with no sign of hearing loss whatsoever. My legs were still a bit wobbly but the doctor had said there was no reason why I should not be able to climb trees in a few weeks' time and run about as I had once done. None of us had any idea about what was to come.

CHAPTER TWO

A Child Goes Deaf

My whole family were waiting for me when I got home. As my mother put the brake on the car, the front door was flung open and my two brothers rushed out, followed at a distance by my sister Natasha who was toddling along as best she could. She was wearing her 'best' dress and had brushed her hair specially for my homecoming. She waddled up to me hollering, 'I wanna *beeg* kiss.'

I was carried indoors and seated at the table, one place being respectfully reserved for a huge teddy which the masters of Merchant Taylors' (where my father was Head Master) had clubbed together to give me. I stubbornly refused to be separated from him. My brother Phil sang *Away in a Manger* unasked, rather as one recites the two times table, brushing aside all prompters: 'No crib – I know it – for a bed.'

Later that evening I was put to bed and I remember suddenly realising how tired I was. My mother went to the door and switched off the light but carried on chatting to me for a while with the door half open. I can remember a sensation of pain in my ears and the sudden realisation of a headache and suddenly I could see my mother standing there in the doorway making no noise at all. It seemed ridiculous: I knew she was talking but my ears told me she wasn't. In the meantime my mother got worried about my lack of response and switched the light on again walking towards me as she did so. I then panicked.

My usually sane mother was walking towards me opening and shutting her mouth rapidly for apparently no reason whatsoever. What she saw was a wide-eyed, panic-stricken little daughter on the verge of a tantrum. Neither of us could pinpoint exactly what was wrong.

The following morning my whole family seemed to have caught the 'mysterious disease' which had affected my mother's behaviour so strangely the night before. Even worse the people on the television seemed to have gone down with it as well. I went out to talk to our elderly gardener but he was the same – my mother could not understand why I kept on crying and refused to allow myself to be touched. She placed me in front of the television again that afternoon in the hope that I would then feel more relaxed after half an hour of Mickey Mouse & Co., but she could see that I hardly responded at all. It was not until she noticed that I kept trying to turn the volume up to deafening levels that she suddenly realised what might have happened.

The following morning I was put into the car and taken back to Mount Vernon Hospital despite my protests. Suddenly I found myself gazing into the normally smiley face of my doctor: only this time he was not smiley at all. He looked distinctly worried and kept patting me on the head. I was taken off to the same room where I'd had a test done on the morning of my discharge from hospital and the audiometric test was repeated. Because I'd had a few of these done before, during my stay in hospital, I knew that I had to put a coloured brick into a wooden box every time I heard a noise. Only this time I seemed to put fewer coloured bricks into the wooden box. In fact, it seemed I had only put a couple in instead of the usual twenty or so, before I felt the headphones being taken off my head, meaning that the test was over. A lady whom I remember wearing a bright red dress under her white jacket looked worried, picked me up and carried me back to my mother. This time the room was full of people all of whom I recognised from some stage of my stay in hospital. They all kept shaking their heads and shrugging their shoulders while I played quietly in the corner. They all seemed to be opening and shutting their mouhs meaninglessly but I had since become resigned to the fact that all people except me had been affected by some strange disease which was making them act in this abnormal manner. As long as they did not hurt me, I had little to fear from them, I decided. My smiley doctor kept flicking through a file of papers and scratching his head with a worried, strained look on his face. Finally he snapped the file shut, sank back in his chair and gave a gesture of helplessness. At this point the other people all began to leave the room, looking at me in a way which suggested they felt sorry for me for some reason which still escaped me. My mother looked upset. I recognised the face of someone who was just about to burst into tears. Slowly she got up and shook the doctor's hand. Then she took my hand as we walked out to the car and, as if in a daze, she drove home. It had come as a shock to her to learn that her daughter had become – overnight – profoundly deaf, with approximately one hundred decibel loss of hearing in both ears. And as she watched my shock, puzzlement and incomprehension she remembered the time when she, as an adolescent, was catapulted into a small, adult French family who had promised her mother to teach her French by never speaking English. My mother knew how I felt.

People spoke too fast so that I couldn't distinguish the words; they turned their heads away and I couldn't understand them at all. When I replied, words completely plain to me were incomprehensible to them. I hardly dared to speak. I slept late and day-dreamed in my room. I wandered around, a lonely and acutely self-conscious observer. I was completely miserable. Yet my mother as a teenager had become fluent in French, as she began to make sense afresh of a new way of communicating. Slowly, word by word, she had become able to reply and was reassured that the French family wanted to laugh with her and not at her. Gradually she had become happy again. This is what she longed would happen to me: she longed that I would learn to speak again, for communication through words is the most basic therapy for the problems of adjustment which all deaf children have and this task was what she set out to fulfil.

It is difficult to explain the changes which my deafness brought about. It changed the whole mentality with which other people approached me. I can quote from an extract from one of my mother's letters to a friend of hers:

> I can always remember going to Northwood in the car with Jessica aged just four and thinking how marvellous it was to be able to talk to such a unique and captivating daughter and six months later no talk at all. The thing is that she doesn't realize yet what a social and psychological (as well as physical) handicap she has. Her deaf-

ness is like an opaque veil which drives me almost frantic with longing for her to read, to communicate and develop this incredible potential.

An extract from another letter to the same friend says:

> Life proves that a weak person must be a loser. If deaf people are isolated amongst hearing people due to their inability to communicate they'll always feel weaker and worse than the others. No wonder therefore some deaf people prefer staying amongst the same unhappy ones – but I will *not* stand aside and allow this to happen to Jessica. She *will* learn to communicate and lead as normal a life as possible. Apart from difficulties with her hearing I dare to say that she *is* normal. She will eventually have the same mentality as any adolescent. She will be faced with the same difficult patches as well as many other teenage girls. In the emotional sphere she will experience almost the same sentimental problems and experience at least the same emotional problems as them in overcoming certain difficulties and hang ups. What she needs therefore is only her rights and not a lot of misunderstanding.

It is extracts like these which, when I read them now, show me just how much my parents must have suffered the colossal shock of having a deaf child in their midst. All parents are anxious, no matter if their child is a boy or a girl, that it is normal and not handicapped mentally or physically in any way at all. When the child is not normal, it appears to the parents as if their world suddenly comes crashing down around them. They may even, worst of all, feel a sense of guilt and shame, or feel responsible for it having happened.

Later, after I had learned how to speak again, I noted that my mother often looked sad. I would suddenly catch her looking at me wistfully with a strange, far away expression in her eyes. Often she cried. After I learned to communicate, I would ask her if she had 'a hurt' – could I kiss it better? I remember that after

I could speak and lipread I asked her, 'Mum, why are you so sad?' My mother answered, 'Because you can't hear.' I told her, 'It doesn't matter Mum, don't be sad, I will be good at school and you will be happy. I have many friends, they all understand me and we play a lot of games together.'

Yet how could my mother accept the innocent logic of my explanation? She fully realised implications of my handicap which I was far too young to appreciate. Once, when I was six-and-a-half she tried to explain to me gently that I was deaf and that deafness could be a serious disability. Yet even this did not affect me. The next day I marched home from Sunday school and said to her, 'God made me deaf 'cos he knew I could cope with it.'

The first problem my mother encountered after I went deaf was my total loss of confidence in speech. I could speak before I went deaf but I had to suffer the colossal shock of becoming deaf which almost eliminated my speech. I had gone very deaf indeed. My parents knew that the great thing was to keep me talking – 'What?' was the first word I learned to lipread. They then trod a delicate path between understanding quickly enough of what I said to make me feel I could communicate and correcting my pronunciation enough for me to be understood by everyone else. But it was not all as straight-forward as it sounds. To make correction acceptable, you must first align yourself with the deaf child – not always an easy task. Unless I learned to accept guidance I would not say words accurately and people would not be able to understand me. This would not be my fault: it was just a boring essential difficulty of being deaf, and dealing with it had to become as habitual and fundamental as brushing my teeth or sharpening my pencils. As I became more confident, my parents tightened up their standards; the attractive mispronunciations of childhood are luxuries the deaf child cannot afford (although my mother confessed to me later that it went to her heart to banish errors such as 'my legs were all *wallaby* when I was in *hostipital*'). Later, after my return to school, my teachers co-operated marvellously over this and gave my mother lists of words that proved intractably difficult such as 'Ghana' and 'diguise'. The way I was taught pronunciation in English was by rhyme. 'Disguise' for instance rhymes with 'miss' and 'lies'. My mother would get the odd consonant changed – the 'L' and the 'G' for instance, if they didn't quite fit, and then finish up with the stress 'disguise'. In English one mostly stresses by emphasis rather than by pitch as in, for instance, Scandinavian languages. I was taught stress by tapping out the rhythm with a pencil. The stress was considered by my mother to be very important. The wrong stress made a word more incomprehensible than the wrong pronunciation. I have reason to believe now that little matters more to a deaf person's success than clear speech, no matter what lengths one has to go to in order to obtain it. My mother turned it into a game of skill, luring the awkward word into conversation, rewarding the effort that pronounces it so well and making me realise that it was worth while not only because it makes speech intelligible but because words in their own right are varied, interesting things.

It should be beginning to be clear now that the basic problem I had to cope with was not that I could not hear but that communication between myself and others was difficult. Learning to communicate presents deaf people in general with increased problems. There are two main, fundamental things which can help the deaf child and his parents in developing the child's ability to communicate. First there is equipment such as a hearing aid, and secondly there is education – things like use of lipreading.

Take hearing aids first, for virtually all deaf children do have some hearing and a hearing aid can amplify whatever sounds they are able to receive. However, it must first be made clear that even the best hearing aid has its limitations. Many people expect a hearing aid to do for a hearing loss what spectacles do for defective vision. Spectacles make vision normal for the wearer. A hearing aid does not restore normal hearing to its user. It can only amplify what the person can already hear. Thus, if they hear only low-pitched sounds and not high-pitched sounds, they will continue to hear low-pitched sounds only, but this will be louder. Also, a hearing aid does not necessarily allow selection of certain sounds. By this I mean, a hearing person can hear his name across a crowded room when in fact it may have been no louder than any other name that was mentioned. This does not happen with a hearing aid: all sounds are picked up and none are filtered out. This is another problem.

The way in which a young deaf child is handled by therapists, doctors, etc. is of vital importance since gaining the patient's confidence is part of the treatment. Social integration, with the help of or by use of hearing aids and lipreading, is what could be called the cure. I was sent to the Heston Clinic run by Dr. Bisch (himself a specialist of many years' standing in children's deafness) under the Hounslow Borough Health Department. This clinic was modern, purpose-built and a teaching and training unit. It was a centre of a district audiology service which was extremely competent and comprehensive. Surely this is one of the best ways in which to tackle the problems of deaf children. It was, for instance, immeasurably more accurate and approachable than the same system run by the same doctor operated within the confines of a large children's hospital. My mother once gave me a very simple example of this.

As I approached the age of five I became increasingly frightened of doctors and hospitals. I was taken to Great Ormond Street to an ordinary clinic three times and I refused point-blank to do an audiometric test. I was issued with a Medresic hearing aid after having had an earmould impression made while my mother held me still because I was screaming. The earmould did not fit, the hearing aid was not nearly strong enough to cope with my degree of deafness and the feedback from the badly fitting earmould was so deafening they couldn't turn it high enough to produce any sound for me at all. I remember thinking the whole thing mad, unpleasant and useless and I became increasingly cross and dejected.

When I was referred to the Heston Clinic, however, my mother was sent an illustrated leaflet showing what would happen so she was able to explain it all to me. She was encouraged to bring my brothers and sisters along. No one was in a hurry. The audiologist let the other children try the headphones on for the test. We had four appointments before I was persuaded to do a test and I eventually had another earmould impression taken to which I consented without tears or struggling. I was then given an earmould that fitted well and an extra-loud hearing aid. I also became immeasurably less upset than I had been before.

Yet the clinic in the hospital and the Heston Hearing Clinic were run by the same doctor. It was the work in the clinic and the patience and quality of the staff there which made the difference. I now had a hearing aid and could therefore be expected to begin to learn how to lipread. Yet to get me to wear my hearing aid every day took some doing.

At first it was no problem at all. My younger brother got me to play with it by pretending to play Z-cars with me just as he had done before I went deaf. He had a small radio with an earpiece, but my 'walkie-talkie' looked much more sophisticated. After a while, however, the novelty wore off and I used to take my aid out from time to time and hide it in order to avoid wearing it. My mother would then not allow me to have any supper until I fetched it and wore it with it switched on. One of my favourite hiding places was at the back of the fridge or down my father's large Wellington boots. This method of evasion did not work, however, and I decided to employ a more direct method of action.

One day I marched in from playing with my friend, hearing aid in hand. I placed it firmly on the table in front of my mother and announced defiantly, using my idiosyncratic sign language, that my episode with my hearing aid was well and truly over. I refused to wear it ever again. I argued that the other children I played with did not have to wear hearing aids: therefore why should I?

I believe that many deaf children use this argument. My mother dealt with it in the only way that was really possible at the time. I could not lipread or speak well enough at this stage so I could not communicate with her enough for her to explain to me *why* I had to wear it. She put it on me and strapped it onto my back, where I could not get at it. When I struggled, I was smacked. If I ever tried to take it off I was smacked again. On the other hand, when I did wear it, my mother smiled at me and cuddled me to her so I soon accepted this 'on means good, off means bad' idea. Once, long after I had been put to bed, I came downstairs for a cuddle. My mother frowned and motioned me to go back upstairs. So I ran back to my bedroom and re-appeared seconds later, all smiles, with my hearing aid on, hoping this would make my mother 'smiley and cuddly' again. It worked, much to my delight, so I often repeated it. In despair my mother was then forced to take my aid away from me when I was put to bed and not let me set eyes on it again before morning.

As I got older and became more able at communication, my mother was able to explain to me more fully why I had to wear my aid. 'Your Nana has a handicap in her eyes, so she wears glasses. So and so has a handicap in his hair, so he wears a wig (but you mustn't let him know I told you). You have a handicap in your ears, so you wear a hearing aid.' I accepted this but I caused embarrassing problems later on for my mother, when I tried to pinpoint other people's handicaps. While out shopping with my mother I pointed to a very fat cashier and announced loudly to my mother, and to everyone else nearby, that she had a handicap in her tummy. Exit one very red-faced mother dragging along a very surprised child.

My mother then had to explain to me the meaning of the word 'tact'. She explained that some people did not like their handicaps pointed out to them so clearly. Nor were they always keen to discuss it either. I tried very hard but I found it difficult to distinguish between the concepts of 'always telling the truth' and 'tact'. Surely one always had to tell the truth? One was not allowed to lie? Therefore tact was lying, was it not? My mother told me that I should never lie but that some things were best left unsaid.

This seemed to work until one day we went to lunch with another family. They lived in Seabrook in a minute house in a chaotic state. It was warm and friendly, however, and there were two extremely pleasant girls who took over my sister Natasha and me, and played with us for the whole day. At the end of it, the mother asked me if I had enjoyed myself and would I like to come again? I replied truthfully in ringing tones: 'I don't like your home but I do like your girls so I would like to come again thank you very much, but I don't like your boy much, and neither do his sisters!' You can imagine how embarrassed my mother must have felt, but fortunately the family found it rather funny. I was nearly six at the time and nobody minds much when children are that age and learning. One overlooks the verbal indiscretions and even finds it amusing when a small child announces to anybody listening, 'I was naughty, I did pooh in my pants.' It is up to the parents, on the other hand, to convince the deaf child of the unwisdom of such remarks. An eight-year-old who blurts out, 'You're fat,' is only embarrassing and offensive – not a bit amusing.

Once I had accepted wearing my hearing aid and was using it properly, my mother began to teach me how to lipread and to read books as well as furthering my pronunciation. This was an area of great struggle which deserves a whole chapter in its own right.

CHAPTER THREE

A Pattern of Lips

Learning how to lipread proficiently was harder than pronunciation. I found it very boring and frustrating and I felt completely cut off from my mother for quite a time. Looking back now, I think the best thing my mother did was to go on reading aloud to me stories which subconsciously I already knew by heart. From this my mother progressed to telling again the stories which I knew the plot of, like Cinderella and Snow White, and then to talking or reading every night for half an hour when I was in bed. At one time I used to dread the evening because I felt so tired and could hardly bring myself to pick up the burden of frustration again at the end of the day. It was then that my mother had a visit from an American social worker who gave her the best advice she'd ever had on teaching me to lipread. The social worker told her to 'put half an hour a day aside for face to face conversation like piano practising' – and it worked wonders.

I think that when normal hearing children are learning to speak, they watch their mothers' faces and mouths as well as listen to their voices. I learnt to lipread by regressing to this stage and began to equate lipreading with hearing. I used to say, 'If you don't turn the light on, I can't hear you'. I also set a lot of store by people's expressions since that very often conveys the matter of the subject under discussion. I would ask my mother, 'How would you look if you were astonished?' 'How would you look if you were telling a funny story?' 'What would your expression be if you were asking me a worried question?' 'How would you look if you were telling me somebody had died?' The other very important thing to remember is that you must look at a deaf person when they are speaking to you as well as when you are speaking to them. Firstly it will encourage their confidence in speech and secondly they will be able to judge by your expression just how much effect what they are saying is having upon the person they are speaking to.

The art of encouraging communication is to find short, easily lipread words like 'soon', 'yes' (accompanied by a nod), 'how nice', 'good', that can be used to keep a conversation going. Lipreading is really a sort of speedwriting – you leap from key word to key word – and then from key phrase to key phrase. The longer the sentence, the harder it is, but my mother always made sure that I got the key words or phrases so that I could at least get the thread and maintain an interest. Lipreading is something which can and must be learnt and although strange faces can confuse it, it is amazing how accurate it can become. By the time I was nearly six, I knew that Natasha said 'ni' and not 'nice' – I even noticed the difference when my brother Philip's two front teeth came out and he couldn't say 'th'. By the time I was eight I could pick up foreign accents, e.g. the French do not say the last letter at the end of a word, e.g. 'down' is 'dow' when pronounced by a French person. Further, the French do not stress certain syllables in a word as much as the English do, e.g. 'óbjĕct' and 'ŏbjéct' are two completely different words in English, the former meaning 'a thing', the latter meaning 'to refuse – to stand against'. One is a noun, the other a verb and this difference is afforded by the whereabouts of the stress. The French speak in equisyllable words e.g. 'téléphoné', where the stress is evenly divided between all four syllables of the word – and one can pick this up by lipreading. I also learnt to recognise Americans by lipreading, as more often than not they run their words into each other! My mother was later to write to a friend: '. . . Jessica can understand accent and dialect and I can't really see why she shouldn't learn foreign languages in due course.'

When I became deaf I had just begun to reach out into the great world of imagination. Fairy stories, historical stories, stories of other lands and other people were all beginning to interest me; suddenly I was totally deprived. I couldn't yet read and I couldn't be read to and I couldn't lipread well enough to find out through conversation. I became seriously bored. There were lots of things I could do to fill in the day like playing games or running races or helping in the house or building houses in the sandpit, but I was cut off from new facts and new ideas. This was the moment that comics came into their own and from them my mother and

I experimented with the whole idea of using pictures – it was like a demented twenty questions. I put all the questions about what was going on in the pictures while my parents gave monosyllabic or shortly phrased answers. In the same way my mother started to teach me to read. I remember one evening my mother was trying to teach me the word 'can' and in sheer desperation she went out into the garden to get a watering can – she wrote out 'watering can', made me say the two words and then finally crossed off the first one.

Yet whichever method you use with reading – 'look and say', 'phonetics' or 'word building' – sooner or later the parent faces a crisis of confidence: 'can she [the deaf child] teach me a word I don't know?' Similarly, I too became worried and felt, 'Shall I *ever* learn to read?' Yet, at first it does not matter what method one uses, the only thing is that you have *got* to get the word across somehow. My mother told me later that she felt reading was by far the most important and rewarding skill to teach a deaf child. I found it fiendishly difficult to learn (as would most deaf children) since I had no memory of the sound of the word I was so laboriously spelling out to jog my comprehension. A hearing child learns 'sun' and thinks 'oh I remember the sun' and half expects the next word to be 'shines'. The deaf child learns that 'sun' sounds like 'son' and thinks 'what is the sun?' By contrast, arithmetic seems simple and relaxing to them.

So we duly plodded on, my parents and I, not realising the enormous dividends it would bring. Once the imaginative vacuum was filled and the boredom ended, not only the answers but also the questions began to come pouring out. This learning was all a very gradual process and although the teaching was started almost as soon as my deafness was diagnosed, I did not really begin making much progress at all until my fifth birthday; after this, it accelerated with leaps and bounds. Until then, I had found the idea of language confusing. I found it difficult to correlate words written down with actual objects and furthermore I could not link objects and spoken words with lip movements. Although I knew that a word was part of a sentence, I could not realise that any one word had a *meaning*. For instance, I did not fully realise that a key was the name only given to an object used to unlock a door with. Furthermore, I could not understand that the word 'key' was used to give that object a separate permanent identity. I could not grasp that the word 'key' was a noun belonging only to keys and not, say, to 'cushions' (i.e. a 'cushion' cannot be called a 'key'). The whole concept – simple as it seems – was alien to me; there was a serious mental block which was retarding my development. My mother would give me a comb and say 'comb' and try to get me to pronounce it properly, but I could not understand that her lip movements, the object in my hands, the word I was struggling to say properly, and the written word COMB were all the *same* thing and not four separate objects. I could not understand what my mother was getting at and although I tried hard, I felt cut off from her and totally miserable. Even if I grasped that a comb was what you used to brush your hair with, how could one then explain the comb on the chicken's head or the concept of beach combing? And what were the teeth of a comb if I was to understand I had teeth in my mouth for eating? I could not make sense of the incoming information and it was an impossible task for me to co-ordinate that information to form a meaningful whole. I could not realise that objects were permanent and this inhibited my language development as it is difficult to name an object when it is not understood as having a permanent independent existence.

My fifth birthday came and I had a tea party for a few friends. This was like any other children's party: noisy, boisterous, hectic for the parents trying to organise it, excited children all running round with ice cream etc. all over their chins and hands while grown-ups chased after them to wipe them clean. I played 'Ring a Ring a Roses' and fell down along with the rest of them. When they played musical bumps, I joined in enthusiastically. The only difference was that instead of waiting for the music to come to a halt, I sat down when I got tired of dancing about! No one minded. When you are that age nobody minds. At tea time we all tumbled into the dining room and immediately began gorging ourselves sick with crisps, sweets and other normally forbidden delights. At length the cake was brought in, the curtains drawn and the candles lit. Everybody began to sing 'Happy Birthday' as loudly and gloriously as they could – most were out of tune, but the feeling was such that the louder, the better, if not in tuneful accord!

The cake was the centre of attention and it was the shape of the cake which jogged something in the back of my mind. It was made in the shape of a hand with four separate fingers and a thumb and there were five separate nails. In the centre of each nail was a candle all lit up, making five candles in all. In the centre of the hand was a large figure 5 in pink icing. By the side of the cake on the icing board was the word FIVE in iced capital letters and underneath this was a pair of lips partially opened – all in pink icing. Suddenly something clicked. I, Jessica Rees was *five* years old. '*Five*' was also the number of fingers and thumbs I had on each hand. I had *five* nails and each candle showed one year for each year I had lived making *FIVE* in all. These figures were *the same as* the word 'Five' written by the side – it was just a different way of presenting a word. The word 'five' *did* have a meaning. I had *five* fingers, *five* nails, I was *five* years old. The iced lips showed that the word could be spoken and understood verbally as well as in its written form. Suddenly it was as if somebody had turned the light on in a dark room. I suddenly realised that all those 'meaningless' mouth movements my mother had been making at me these last months and all those letters she had written down in groups as single words were in fact not meaningless at all. They were all the names given to separate objects in order to give them a form of identification. I realised that although nails, fingers, my age and a written word could seem to have nothing in common at all, they could all be linked by one word – FIVE. Furthermore, I realised that the magic word did not have to be 'five', it could be anything under the sun. It was like being electrocuted: I stood rooted to the spot in this sudden flash of realisation. I felt as Helen Keller must have felt when she stood at the pump while Annie Sullivan operated it and water gushed all over her hands. I felt as elated as she must have felt when she suddenly realised that water was the name given to a wet, slippery liquid which you could also drink and not to anything else. I, too, grasped that objects were unique and the names given to these objects were also unique.

I grabbed a biscuit and ran to my mother, thrust it in her

hand and said 'What?' A puzzled look came over her face. I picked up a pencil and a piece of paper from nearby and repeated 'What? Write it.' She spelt out BISCUIT on the paper and slowly formed the word with her lips. She then finger spelt it and to her amazement I said 'Biscuit' word perfectly. I then said 'Biscuit . . . you eat biscuit if here (and I pointed to my tummy) goes rumble rumble', She pointed to what she had written and I repeated 'biscuit'. She then wrote underneath 'cake'. I said, 'No – that is not biscuit, biscuit is what you wrote there' . . . and in saying so I pointed to it.

By this time the other children had blown out my candles for me, impatient with waiting, and the cake had been cut up and was in the process of disappearing, which is an elegant way of saying the children were gobbling it up as fast as they could. My mother fetched a piece of cake and pointed to it and then to the word 'cake' on the paper and said 'cake'. It was clear to me now what she meant. I pointed to the cake she was holding, then to the written word 'cake', nodded vigorously and said 'cake'. I then pointed to my biscuit and then to the written word 'biscuit', nodded again and said 'biscuit'. My mother pointed to the written word 'cake' and then pointed at my biscuit and raised her eyebrows questioningly waiting . . .

'Silly Mummy', I said and smacked her, 'Wrong, bad', 'cake is *cake*', I said pointing to the cake and to the written word 'cake'. 'Cake is *not* biscuit' I said and added in a know-all way. 'They *not* the *same*.' I could not understand what all the fuss was about.

From then on my progress rocketed and by the following week I had a lipread and spoken vocabulary of over 100 extra words. I still made mistakes however, one of the funniest was to do with a Christmas carol which I picked up by lipreading when I was 8. My mother soon realised I was singing 'We wish you a merry xmas and a happy two new ears!' Irony of the highest order!

I was lucky, as for me the penny finally dropped, but the more you think about it, the more terrifying the implications of deafness in a child become. Deafness is the one handicap which if present, alone, in a child can prevent total intellectual and emotional development, which no other handicap alone can do.

S.S.S.–B

For those who have never encountered a young deaf child, it is hard to understand how much difference it can make. One might think of what a person misses who cannot hear music, church bells or the birds' singing. One might think of the practical problems of having a young deaf child that does not hear cars coming or a horn hooting; that one cannot call out to warn of danger and so one has to keep him close. But it is *not* these things that constitute the real problem of deafness. Life can be less meaningful without the joys that sounds can bring and there are situations which can be dangerous for someone who cannot hear. But there are greater problems than these. It is learning to comprehend other people and to communicate with them that is the real area of difficulty. The deaf child with limited or even no understanding of what is said to him and not being able to talk himself can be cut off in many ways from what goes on around him.

You can compare deafness and blindness in children. Blindness cuts people off from things, but deafness cuts people off from other people. There is no question whatsoever that early life and childhood for the child born blind are much more normal than they are for the child born deaf. The blind child has far more contact and understanding of the world about him. We initially learn more through our ears than we do our eyes. The blind child has no problem of communication. Further, his handicap is obvious – there is no question of it remaining undiagnosed for any length of time. It is not only obvious – it is immediately obvious. Strangers look at the child and see he is blind. There is immediate compassion and immediate help. Deaf children are deprived of these advantages. The deaf child looks normal, but in fact his handicap is very real.

The most famous deaf and blind person of our age, Helen Keller, herself said that 'The problems of deafness are deeper and more complex than those of blindness. Deafness is a much worse misfortune. For it means the loss of the most vital stimulus – the sound of the voice that brings language, sets thoughts astir, and keeps us in the intellectual company of man.' But there is no doubt that the ultimate adjustments and levels of attainment that can be achieved by the deaf child can be greater than the ultimate adjustments of the blind. The very fact that deafness is not visible (even though it can make life so hard for those people suffering from it) means that the deaf can become more easily accepted as part of society than one whose handicap is visually obvious.

After that day when I suddenly recognised what was happening I realised that the facial gestures centred on people's mouths were accompanied by the sounds I had once heard and were used to effect communication, to express feelings, desires, frustrations, anger, in fact anything. I grasped the rudiments of what my mother was trying to teach me, and I began learning more and more words every day. These new words led to the explanation of new ideas like 'What is a comet?' 'I am a viking coming across the sea to get you' – and a re-entry into the world of thoughts and ideas. My mother was consciously trying to widen my vocabulary and she told me later that the easiest way to do this was to stop herself whenever she felt she was trying to translate something into easily recognised words. She would ask herself 'What word are you avoiding?' It may have been 'Pakistan' or possibly 'transport' or even 'in spite of'. She would make herself stop and explain it. If she found it difficult to pin down the meaning exactly, she would pin it down by usage (often usage is the best way of helping a child to memorise words anyhow). Once she was explaining 'in spite of' and she told me that it meant the same as 'even if'. She said to me, 'I should eat your flap jacks in spite of them being burnt'. (I knew this wasn't true) – we then had a long wrangle which ended up with 'I am telling the truth in spite of what you say'. Words such as 'Pakistan' or 'transport' were easier, e.g. Pakistan as a country, who lives there, Pakistanis living in England, the whole question of race relations, test matches etc., endless possibilities. The other way of enlarging vocabulary was by grabbing new facts and ideas and talking about them. Another example of this would be if my brothers started to talk about football at teatime (well that hardly rated as a new topic but it is a good example!), my mother would expect me to have learnt 'referee', 'half time', 'score', 'FA Cup', 'rugger', etc.; by the end of it. It is a mistake to cram in too many words at once, however, since one also has to explain the sense, check the sound, and stress the emphasis and usage. I loved words, as many deaf children do, and I loved poetry. If you talk to yourself you are usually thought to be slightly mad, but if you recite poetry, nobody minds. Poetry does deaf children so much good too in a practical way, as it automatically makes them stress the word and phrases correctly. From 'Mary, Mary quite contrary' to 'shall the multitudinous seas incarnadine; Making the green, one red'. Poetry explains and points the words it uses. It juxtaposes sound and rhyme very obviously and gives direct to the mind of the deaf child some of the pleasure which hearing people have relayed to them all day through their ears. The only element of poetry which is perhaps denied to deaf children is the poetry of sound. When such phrases as 'the *crackling* of the fire' or 'the *rustle* of the wind in the trees' or 'the *crunching* of footsteps in the snow' are used as hearing adjectives to describe sounds, they are infuriatingly meaningless to a deaf person who has no memory of sounds at all (and doesn't even know what the word 'sounds' means). Even trying to describe the nature of a particular sound to me is like trying to describe the colour blue to a person who is totally blind. It is impossible both for the person trying to describe it and for me to grasp the idea. It is virtually hopeless trying to imagine what a sound is like when you have had literally no memory of any sound for 15 years. I do not know how ANY words are sounded – even verbs or pronouns. Mentally I see words in the printed form or in finger spelling. I never think of them phonetically. I do not possess oral thinking even though I am quite capable of speech. Whenever I do any light reading such as Wodehouse's books about Jeeves the butler, pictures are the predominant features that appear in my mind.

Nevertheless, this did not stop me reading what poetry I could when I was small, and as the weeks went by my mother started to introduce me to papers and magazines as well as comics. She was brought up in a family which believed so much in books that they never threw any way – that was a sin – and would be quite happy in doctors' waiting rooms if they could read outdated copies of Bradshaws Railway timetable.

In a few months, my progress was judged satisfactory enough for me to start at kindergarten school again at Easter after a gap of several months. Yet this re-entry into the hearing world was only to be one of the several hurdles which I would face in my lifetime. I had left the kindergarten in November because of my illness, having started there only in September. Before my illness, my speech and aural comprehension of other people had been beginning to develop. After I'd gone deaf my speech had nearly been eliminated and it still needed constant care – it was by no means 'normal' speech at this stage. My aural comprehensions had been well and truly obliterated and I'd had to start all over again learning to lipread from scratch. My contemporaries were now way ahead of me in educational and social development. I could read and write now enough to be able to keep up with them, but even with special teaching one can never provide the vast experience the hearing child has of spoken communication.

I was lucky that the children in my class had known me in September onwards, before I went deaf in November, and had played with me and treated me like any normal friend. When I'd gone ill, they'd all gone through it with me. They'd visited me in hospital, had drawn me pictures, kept me informed of what was going on and in the early stages of my hospital stay when I had been in a coma, they had been informed every morning in assembly as to how I was and together they had all prayed for me. When I'd gone deaf, the teacher explained to the class that I could not hear any more and that they would now all have to act as my ears and to allow me to be as normal as possible. Yet children at this age are very adaptable and they still thought of me as the Jessica they'd known before and *not* as a deaf child, i.e. they thought of me as a person and related my achievements to me as a person, *not* to my condition. Hence, when I returned to school feeling a bit shy, awkward, lost and lonely, not knowing what to expect, I found them all waiting for me, each one wanting to hold my hand, to sit next to me in assembly, class, lunch etc., to play with me and to be my friend – my worries, and those of my mother, vanished immediately.

CHAPTER FOUR

I Get a Baby Sister

It was not long before life settled down to normal again and I was back to my usual mischievous form. My teachers must have begun to despair when a boy and I got busy in the sandpit building a dam by means of which (and with the help of the school's garden hose) we managed to flood the entire junior cloakroom area, not to mention a bit of the kitchen area where perishable goods were stored.

Television lessons posed a problem at first, but we overcame this eventually: I was lent the teacher's handbook the night before. But even then it caused slight havoc as the next morning upon my arrival at school, I would immediately gather all my friends around me and tell them *exactly* what the TV programme we were going to see later that day was about, *exactly* who said what to whom and *exactly* 'what happened in the end'! When we were shown the film later on in the day, the teacher would say something like, 'Now watch this film carefully and I want you especially to notice what sort of food poor people in Victorian England used to eat.' She would be somewhat disconcerted when a pupil would immediately pipe up, 'Please Miss, the poor people in this film eat nothing much apart from black bread and dripping and, please Miss, it looks REVOLTING'. Upon which the whole class would nod their heads in agreement and pull faces of revulsion.

My friends all helped me in little ways. One boy called Ian (the same one who helped me to build the aforementioned dam) would sit beside me in class while the teacher read aloud. He would obtain a copy of the book beforehand and throughout the reading session he would point to the words in the book as the teacher read them out, hence (1) integrating me with the rest of the class and not isolating me and (2) enabling me to keep pace with the reading rate of the rest of the class. The teacher did not ask him to do this, he simply made up his own mind about how to help me and got on with it. I had another friend called Susan who also helped me a lot. For example, every time a teacher started talking anywhere, she would manoeuvre me round to face the teacher and, if necessary, she would march hand in hand with me to the front of the class where I could see better. Everybody needs friends, but we, the deaf, need them more than most people. We need good friends that we can trust and whom we know that we can go to for help. The children at Miss Maycock's never teased me about my hearing aid, they just accepted it as part of me. They seldom, if ever, made any passing reference to my disability or my slow, unsteady speech. Most of them didn't dare! Ian who was my staunch friend was also the registered class bully!

Having a sense of humour was also very important to me at that time. I'll always remember one occasion when Ian, Susan and I were playing around in the playground after lunch. It was a very wet June day and pouring with warm, wet, soft rain. We were all dressed up in our wellingtons and mackintoshes complete with bright yellow sou'wester hats and we were merrily splashing around in puddles getting more and more boisterous and more and more mucky. Susan suddenly stopped and took hold of my hand saying, 'Don't you think your hearing aid might get dirty? Why don't you take it off for now and give it to the teacher?' Ian exploded laughing and said, 'Why should she? Wearing a hearing aid stops water getting in your ear if it rains!'

Trouble arose one day when the teacher tried to explain to the class the concept of 'before' or 'after'. The idea of past, present and future, the ideas that some things may not happen now but will be possible in the future. I found things in the future very difficult to understand and it was difficult for my mother to explain them to me. I could not fully comprehend statements like 'After dinner we'll go out' etc. I only understood what I happened to be doing at the present moment. This would often cause problems for my mother when I was out at my friend's house for tea, enjoying myself tremendously until my mother would say it was time to go, because it was late and Natasha needed to be put to bed. She couldn't say to me 'Come on Jessica, we've got to go home now. You can come back tomorrow.' She could only say, 'Come on Jessica, we're going now' and I wouldn't want to go. To me, it seemed that I *had* to go and was never coming back as far as I was concerned – it was difficult for my mother to explain that I could come back sometime in the future. (It is often the reassurance that he can come back another time which induces a child to come away even if he does not want to go home. But it may not be possible to get this across to the deaf child.) It would often hurt my mother because she couldn't explain *why* I couldn't do certain things and why I had to do other things. She often couldn't give me any reasons – just had to tell me to get on with it.

Looking forward to Christmas, birthdays and holidays is an exciting part of a young child's life once they are old enough to appreciate the special air of such an occasion. I was on the verge of realising this when I went deaf and for a while afterwards it was difficult to explain to me that something exciting was going to happen. If my mother wrote Christmas cards to send off, I would think it was a birthday. Also it was very difficult for her to explain the 'Christmas is a-coming and the geese are getting fat' idea to me as I could not detect the atmosphere of excitement which largely originated from the excited tones in which my brothers and sisters whispered to each other. Being deaf, I could not comprehend what was going on. Likewise, trying to recall the immediate past was difficult. My mother could not say to me, 'Can you remember what happened in Northwood the other day?' It led to confusion. There was an occasion once when my father's mother, Nana, was staying with us and she started to talk to me about a little game that she and I had played at in her house at Sunderland. It consisted mainly of a type of hide and seek game whereby I would hide her wooden spoon. She tried to say, 'Do you remember when you hid my wooden spoon in the oven?', but I thought she meant we were going up to Sunderland now to stay with her so that we could play the game again. After lunch my mother found me with my suitcase ready packed and my teddy bears all ready to go – which was awful. I was very upset and my mother had to raid her Christmas presents to try and console me. She couldn't make me understand the concept of 'do you remember?', not even 'yesterday'. I thought that whatever happened that was being spoken about meant that we were going to do it now. I could not bring the past into the present nor project the present into the future.

At first sight, not being able to talk about the past and the future may not seem an overwhelming problem, but it is these sorts of conversations that enable a child to see life as continuous and structured. Christmas day, instead of being a climax of wrapping presents and putting up decorations can seem an isolated day. More important, if the deaf child is out playing or at school, as I was, and is unable to tell his mother about what he has been doing, his day may become divided into isolated segments for him as it did in my case. Communication is not just the imparting of information but has a wider significance in that it is a way of maintaining contact and continuity.

My mother got round the problem by pinning up a large poster of a calendar on my bedroom wall. Each room was separated from the others by thick black lines and was divided up into days by means of seven columns representing the seven days of the week. Every night as she put me to bed, she and I would cross off the present day and put a ring round the following day. This was the last thing I did every night. This way I slowly grasped the idea of the year as a continuous process unfolding slowly day by day. I had only to glance at the crossed off days to see the 'past' time that has been spent, or at the uncrossed days to see the future time that has not been spent. The day with a ring round it was the present, *today* – a single moment in time. She also taught me the 24-hour clock which took some time to sink in, but eventually I began to see each day as part of a continuous cycle.

After this I began to grasp the idea of verb tenses, e.g. the use of past tense and future tense as well as present. Until now I had always written and spoken mainly in the present tense, not understanding the potentials which language offered. It was not long before I transferred to conditional tenses and was using such sentences as 'When I am rich I will feel as if I should give a large amount of it to the poor'.

The former misconception I had about time often led to some amusing situations to say the very least – the day *after* Decimal Day in Great Britain when the metric system of coinage came into use, I went to the school tuckshop and tried to buy some sweets with the old coinage. The gentleman tried to tell me that since yesterday we had 'gone decimal' but I protested loudly saying, '*Yesterday* was decimal day, today is not decimal day any more!' – thinking that it was all right to use the old coinage since decimal day was over. I could not understand that the change to a new decimal system of coinage was intended to be permanent, i.e. extended into the future.

I was by now nearly six years old and my mother was pregnant with Camilla who was later to become the seventh and final addition to our family. I can remember one Saturday in February when my brother Robert had two friends – Andrew and Tommy – to lunch. Tommy was being very funny about why his family was not moving house as had been formerly planned. With all the wisdom of a 7-year old, he explained, 'You see, we aren't very rich, and it doesn't look as if we ever will be. *Such* a large family, and food is *so* expensive and then at night we all queue up outside the bathroom door and use *such* a *lot* of *water*.' My brother Rob replied, 'Well, you're only five – we shall soon be seven!' There was a horrified pause while everyone looked at my mother. I then realised that my mother's stomach had in fact expanded a bit and after lunch I decided to ask her why. I did, and she told me that she was carrying a little baby around inside her which would come out just before my sixth birthday. I became very keen on the idea as many of my friends had little baby brothers or sisters so I looked forward to the birth.

About a week before Camilla was born, however, we had some oranges for lunch one Saturday which were all rotten in the middle. That afternoon, therefore, I went shopping with my mother and we took them back to the greengrocers to see if we could get a refund. My mother explained to me: 'It's not *his* fault the oranges are bad and we mustn't be cross with him, but if you ask him nicely, he might give you some more oranges or your money back.' I grinned and walked into the shop with the plastic bag full of these smelly, rotten oranges and smiled angelically at our friendly greengrocer while my mother stood behind me exchanging winks with him:

'Here,' I said, opening the bag for him, 'Have a sniff.' He bent over and looked.

'Goodness gracious me,' he said. 'They are all black and horrid aren't they?'

'Yes,' I replied calmly, 'We tried to eat them for lunch.'

'I'm extremely sorry madam,' he replied in a friendly 'serious' tone. 'If I'd known they were bad I would not have sold them to you'.

'Do you possibly think we could have our money back?' I asked in my most grown-up voice possible, 'or could we have some more oranges instead?' I looked up anxiously at my mother who mouthed 'You're doing fine' at me and winked.

'Let me see', pondered the greengrocer. 'How many are there, six? OK. Say I give you seven oranges instead. One extra to say I'm sorry and maybe a little present for you as well?'

'Thank you very much,' I said using my best speech. I was thrilled, it had worked! I had achieved something. The greengrocer came back with seven oranges in a clean plastic bag and a little bunch of what he knew to be my favourite grapes in a brown paper bag. He shook my hand solemnly, apologised once more whilst winking broadly at my mother and waved us goodbye out of the shop.

Now I would know in future how to exchange faulty goods in the politest way possible. But in my own little way, I had somehow got the idea that anything was exchangeable – even baby sisters!

A few days later Camilla was born and I was separated from my mother for longer than I had ever been before, while she went into hospital. But it was not too long before we all trooped in to see her to meet the latest addition to our family.

I expected a sweet, sleepy, cute and lovable little baby sister like my friend Susan had, but what a shock I got when I first saw her – she was purple faced and squalling – I was disgusted! Surely *my* mother could do better than that! What was more, she claimed a lot of my mother's attention which I had become used to over the last eighteen months since my illness. I was indignant! The final straw came when I saw her occupy at length what I regarded as *my* place, in my mother's arms. By now I was seething with jealousy, rage and disappointment. My little baby sister to whom I had been looking forward for weeks had proved to be as big a let-down as possible. I decided to register a vigorous complaint.

'Where did she come from?' I demanded to know. My mother looked a bit startled – she obviously thought it was a bit early to begin explaining facts like that to me. 'Why do you ask?' she queried, her eyebrows raised in a somewhat amused fashion.

'Well, if you knew where she came from,' I pointed out in a cross tone, 'we could return her like we did the oranges and get our money back!' My mother explained that this was not possible, but I was adamant. 'What if we ask nicely?' I argued. 'It wasn't the shop's fault she's like this, so we mustn't get cross with them, but . . .' repeating all she'd said to me over the 'bad oranges affair'.

I guessed she was laughing at me and I got upset. I refused to speak any more that day and remained miserable until she came home again with that wretched little bundle in her arms. The afternoon she came home she called me into her room. I went in expecting to have to share her attention with everyone else, especially that little blighter, and entered sulkily. To my surprise she was on her own having got rid of the others a few seconds earlier. Even Camilla was not to be seen. She explained to me that little babies need a lot of looking after and I nodded miserably expecting that I would now see less and less of her, but I was taken aback for she went on to say, 'I can't do it on my own. Will you help me? *We'll* do it *together*. As my eldest daughter you are a big girl now and I need your help.' Suddenly I felt confident and elated again. I nodded vigorously – the change in my behaviour was instant. I immediately became cheerful and co-operative.

'Your first job will be to make sure she is asleep and all right. I'm in bed and can't get out yet, so will you do it for me?,' she asked, pointing to the cot in the corner. I gave the thumbs up sign and tiptoed across the room to look.

Camilla had changed considerably since our first meeting. The redness had gone and a slight pinkiness of the cheeks was all that remained. She was sleeping peacefully and looked sweet, cute – everything I had wanted my baby sister to look and lying there in her cot she looked surprisingly defenceless. This aroused my protective instincts. She was *my* sister and I was going to help look after her.

I looked across the room at my mother and grinned. She gave a sigh of relief. Her worst fears had been avoided.

CHAPTER FIVE

Weather is lovely . . . wish you were here

This chapter is dedicated to Cameron Robert McCracken.

One of the nicest things about being young was the excitement which going away for a holiday caused. Once I had overcome my earlier problem of understanding what was meant by the future and the past, I was able to appreciate the 'air of expectation' which occurred just before our family all went away each summer.

I can't remember much about the early holidays when I was very young except that the journey down to the South of France always involved a string of campsites. The funniest memories I have are of my father struggling to put up our tent while we remained passive onlookers with my mother desperately trying to cook for the whole family on a tiny stove. There would be Natasha hollering for something or other while Philip would be anxiously trying to help everyone (but only getting more and more in the way); Rob and I would wander off exploring and come back, late and dirty, much to my mother's despair.

One of the best things about these holidays was that I was excused my formal speech lessons from start to finish. I only had to accept corrected versions of words I pronounced wrongly and say them right – even this produced problems at times when I insisted that 'petits pois' were pronounced 'pettie pottis' while steak was pronounced 'steek'. 'Steek and ships' became the order of the day, as I could not say 'ch' either.

Because of all the swimming, I was often excused wearing my hearing aid which was an added treat as I was freed from the irritating squealing noises it used to make at times, which led to black looks from my brothers and sisters, and I felt more normal. I was made to wear it after my final swim of the day, however, and all through the evening meal – but somehow I did not mind this. In the same way, my brother enjoyed not having to practise the piano for a while. So between us, we felt we did quite well.

My great uncle had restored a château in the South of France and many of our holidays were spent there at Château des Valettes. It was an ideal place for children. Situated on the side of a valley in the Alpes Maritimes with a swimming pool and extensive grounds complete with vineyards, it was extremely beautiful. My great uncle always made us welcome but he was also quite remote. I remember seeing him at mealtimes in the evenings, when we ate out on the terrace overlooking the valley as the day slowly and gradually faded into night. He usually led the conversation, and from time to time made comments which provoked laughter from the other grown-ups. During the day he was often in his study working, but occasionally we saw him at the pool. I remember always being very much in awe of him. Physically too he could be quite intimidating. He was six feet tall, which to our small frames was huge, with a very striking face crowned with enormous white bushy eyebrows which moved when his face became animated. I can recall one day when my sister and I were reading comics by the side of a lawn and we suddenly looked up to find him in front of us. My first instinct was one of alarm – I couldn't lipread him well enough to converse with him. Luckily Natasha did the talking. He asked how we were and other polite questions. The only sentence I managed to understand him say was 'Are you enjoying this place?' accompanied by a sweeping gesture of his hand at the surroundings. We both nodded vigorously. He seemed pleased by this and put his hand into his pockets pulling out two silver French francs – one each for my sister and me. We were a bit overawed at this and thought him terribly rich to be able to afford what to our young minds was an extremely generous, extravagant gesture. Then just as suddenly as he had come, he waved and left. I watched him walk back across the lawn hardly believing I had a whole franc in my pocket all for me.

Even though holiday times were fun, they were also sometimes a strain. I hated the evening meal when we were in campsites because everyone always carried on talking long after the meal at our little camping table under the trees had ended. This meant that the conversation went on well into the darkness: hence I could not see to lipread any more. I used to get seriously bored at times and go to bed early.

An amusing incident occurred once which caused my parents a great deal of embarrassment as a result of my going-to-bed-early syndrome. We had a camping car which was fixed so that the driver's and the passengers' seats could both be elongated to make two beds, each running the whole length of the car. The bed on the driver's side was shorter on account of the steering-wheel being in the way so I was always made to sleep on this side, while my elder brother Robert slept on the other. One night when I was bored I decided to call it a day and crawled into my sleeping bag and tried to get to sleep. Finding I was hot, I wound down the window on my side hoping it would make the place cooler. I soon realised however that my face was not near enough the window in order for the cooling effect to take place. So I tried to remedy the situation. It was all very simple really: I just grasped my pillow and raised it up till it rested on the steering wheel and then I leant my head back on it. The horn blared out into the whole campsite non-stop while I, completely unaware of what I was doing, nestled down to try and get to sleep again. Suddenly a hand appeared at the open window, grasped my hair and yanked me rudely from my repose and I looked up to find an amazed slightly stunned look on my father's face. My mother collapsed laughing.

This is only one example of just how dangerous I could prove if left to my own devices. There was once a time when I was slightly older, about ten or so, and one morning my mother woke up feeling rather ill. My dad arranged to take her immediately to the nearest hospital which was in Apt, 14 kilometres away. We were camping at the time, on some land in Provence, which was later to be the site of our house, so my father had to leave us all with only the tent and the trees for shelter from the scorching sun and drive off in the car with my mother. He promised not to be too long and told us all to be good. Robert, the eldest, was in charge.

For a while we sat in the tent playing card games away from the wasps, but as the day got hotter and hotter as the sun rose higher, the suffocating heat in the tent became unbearable. The solution we decided, was to look for something else to do. We crawled out and suddenly some bright spark hit upon the idea of building an air raid shelter with all the big stones lying around.

There were some gardening tools nearby and the boys set upon building a deepish hole while the girls collected large enough rocks, Camilla did her bit too, even though she was only four. The very sight of her puffing and panting, trying to shift huge boulders which even Tash and I could not lift by ourselves was highly amusing. She mainly collected what could politely be called pebbles. I got bored pretty quickly with this mundane task and wandered off to pick lavender and read whilst sniffing at the plants' pungent perfume.

I can't remember why but I suddenly went running back to tell Robert something and in doing so I did not notice a rake which lay in my path with the bent area at the tip facing towards me, spikes upwards. It was like something out of a 'Tom and Jerry' cartoon where the cat runs round a corner straight into a rake which tips up and hits him flat in his face. You laugh at it on the screen but you never suspect it will happen to you. I was suddenly hit in the face seemingly from nowhere, I screamed as I fell. My brothers and sisters came rushing up to where I was sprawled screaming my throat out. Tash somehow had a mug of dirty water in her hand which she gave me to drink in a somewhat confused but trying-to-be-helpful manner. Then she changed her mind and started to apply it to my forehead with her fingertips which she dipped into the water at intervals. Of course if anyone touched my head it hurt even more and I screamed angrily at her. They were all looking for any blood and Camilla kept asking if I was dead yet. Philip was terribly worried because Dad had told us all to be good. I didn't give a damn, I was in too much pain to even think of the consequences so when Phil quite rightly pointed out solemnly, 'It would have to happen when Dad is away and Mum is ill', I told him to shut up.

The consequences were that I had an enormous black eye to greet my Dad with on his return late that afternoon. When we went to see Mum in hospital I was able to cheer her up with it, and the whole episode is now a family joke.

For a deaf child, a family holiday can prove to be an excellent means of enlarging vocabulary. My mother used to grasp every available opportunity to feed me with new words. Going through customs was heaven for her – and hell for me. Every five minutes she would point out a word which I had never seen before, make me pronounce it properly and explain its meaning in great detail. We went through the purpose of customs, the meaning and implications of having nothing or something to declare, the green and the red channels, which led on to the whole question of smuggling etc; the possibilities were infinite. The danger of rabies proved highly amusing as I used to get very upset at having to leave our dog at home. I felt it was unfair on her that we should go off and enjoy ourselves while she had to go into kennels. Once just before we boarded the boat my mother told me all about the danger of rabies caused by smuggling animals into Britain and filled me with gruesome details of the symptoms of the disease. I felt quite sick. We then approached an official who motioned to us to stop, and as my mother wound down the windows he asked her to certify she had no animals in the car.

'Only in the back' she replied pointing to us indignant children with a broad grin on her face. He laughed and waved her forward.

Apart from customs and all the formalities concerned with going abroad, my mother opened my eyes to foreign foods, habits and ways of life. These all provided scope for imagination and it broadened my understanding of the ways in which other people live, their culture and their philosophies, all different from our own. It was education in the broadest sense of the word. Education by exposure.

Surely this is one of the best ways of teaching a deaf child. There is an ancient Chinese proverb which says:

Tell me – I forget.
Show me – I remember.
Involve me – I understand.

This is exactly what my mother did. Teaching was done by exposure and involvement. She did not just tell me about Paris and the French, she took me there and we explored it together. She did not just tell me that Chinese people use chopsticks, she took me to a Chinese restaurant and made me use the things. She made me understand the implications of a different way of life, religion or race. Together we went to a Jewish synagogue to see for ourselves how they worshipped the Lord and today I remember these things because I was not just told about them, I was involved and exposed in a way which reinforced my understanding.

CHAPTER SIX

Inside the Deaf Head

All the time day in, day out, I was being educated, not only academically but also socially and psychologically. Deafness is so much a social and psychological, as well as physical, handicap that constant therapy is necessary to maintain the self-confidence of the deaf individual. Without it one becomes unable to consider oneself as a person in one's own right. My education extended way beyond the classroom. I had constant speech lessons and several attempts were made to teach me to make the utmost use of my residual hearing. This bored me to tears. It seemed futile – a complete waste of time. I had to concentrate on my linguistics all the time. As yet my control of language was far from perfect. Every rule, every piece of grammar, every verb, every word had to be painstakingly learnt bit by bit. Once I grasped the basic concept I could usually manage but it was the actual process of grasping the concept which took so long and then there were so many concepts . . .

My language difficulties often led to behaviour problems which is a polite way of saying that I sometimes lost my temper and behaved like a juvenile delinquent. I resented other people's normality and wanted them to suffer difficulties, even if I had to inflict them myself. I once provoked my brother Robert to tears by piling his sardines on top of his ham: he couldn't eat either of them. Obnoxious gestures like this were really motivated by jealousy. At other times I was no trouble at all.

As far as the classroom and problems of adjustment were concerned, things were no easier. The time had come for me to leave Miss Maycock's school and to start at St Helen's, Northwood. I knew this was going to be a tough challenge, and I was only eight years old when I left the cosy atmosphere of my first school to be catapulted into this large girls' high school on the top of Northwood Hill. It was a terrifying experience. None of the girls from Miss Maycock's moved there with me. I was alone, surrounded by strangers – all eight-year-old girls like myself, only they had never seen a deaf child before and had no idea what deafness even was. It was then that the psychological problems really started and I became acutely aware of my deafness and the fact that I was physically different from everyone else. Small deaf children under the age of seven suffer little discomfort – they are usually unaware of the fact that they are handicapped or different until they are intellectually developed enough to accept explanations. At my first school, the children took very little notice of the fact that I was deaf: they just adapted to my needs and accepted me for what I was. At St Helen's, however, the situation was vastly different and I quickly became the victim of a lot of abuse and ridicule. I'm not saying that it was the fault of the school – the school itself was well equipped, well run and the staff were very pleasant and friendly. It was nobody's fault: it was merely ignorance. It was ignorance on the part of the girls who had no idea how to speak to me, ignorance on how to treat me or to realise what my abilities were – to see what I could do and what I couldn't do. In short they were embarrassed by my deafness and simply had no idea how to cope.

On the other side of the coin I had not had to cope with anything like this before. I could not understand why the class of thirty girls kept staring at me and making visual references to my very obvious body-worn hearing aids, with their wires trailing up to my ears. I could not understand why they avoided me when I tried to speak to them and play with them, but it slowly dawned on me day by day that my physical handicap embarrassed them in a way it had never embarrassed anyone before. My slow speech made them impatient and in turn that upset me and made my speech even slower, because I worried so much about it, and it became a vicious circle. I took to playing by myself in a corner of the playground during break and one day I noticed a group of older girls who kept looking at me and talking among themselves. I couldn't understand what they were talking about and so I couldn't join in. They started to tease me about being deaf and dumb, which continued until the teacher on duty stepped in and broke it up, telling them they 'ought to be ashamed of themselves', and at the same time telling me 'not to worry – they just don't understand'. I lasted out the rest of the day, but when I got home I started to cry. My mother said, 'What's the problem?' I said, 'I've no friends to play with and they are teasing me. I don't understand what's wrong with them.' My mother tried to explain to me, but I couldn't believe her. I wanted to make friends with *them*. It seemed as if there was a thick wall between us which was very difficult to break down. Sometimes I felt like telling the world to get lost. Being deaf and therefore disabled was like being chained to something. I couldn't get away from it.

If you are deaf, words are only movements of the lips. *They* watch interesting films on television and you don't understand. *They* hear information on the radio. And you? You aren't very fond of reading because you don't understand all the words. There is not always someone who can help you and translate. Whenever you go to the cinema you must choose a film with plenty of action and subtitles because otherwise you won't understand. Sometimes you are angry because their life seems easier than yours. Sometimes you reflect just why the hell you have to be deaf.

There was even one day when I approached one of those girls, huddled in a group in the playground. She looked friendly. I smiled at her and said in my best voice, 'I like the game you are playing. Please can I join in so that we can become friends?' She took one look at me and said, 'Mummy said I can't play with you because you are deaf.' The fact that I was deaf finally sank in and I grasped the basic implications of my handicap. But even today I find it difficult to get over the sheer impact those words had on me. I remember running away from the group blindly towards the cloakroom, where I could at least escape from their cold stares. I ran in and bumped straight into another girl from my class who was just hanging her coat up.

'Hello,' she said, 'What's the matter?'

I couldn't lipread her, but I was too scared to tell her in case she just gave me an all too familiar exasperated look and walked off. So I just stood there. She didn't seem to mind. She just said it again more slowly, smiling all the time.

'Hello. I'm Clare. Are you all right?' This I grasped and, deciding I liked her, nodded and replied, 'I'm Jessica. I don't like the other girls, but I like you.' Clare waited patiently for me to form my words slowly and nodded encouragingly as I got each word out.

'Cheer up,' she said, 'It's English now. Would you like to sit next to me in class?' She acted out this sentence with gestures and mime to help me lipread her. I nodded and she took hold of my hand and led me into the classroom.

Throughout my two years at St Helen's, it was Clare who stuck by me all the time when the going got rough. She soon established a quick and easy visual means of communication with me and we became really close friends. With her placid, kind nature, she also got on with other girls in the class and was therefore able to act as an intermediary, assuring them that I was 'quite normal really and that there was nothing to worry about'. She was able to explain to me that the other girls weren't really all that horrible. They were just shy and unsure how to behave towards me.

Even though things got better, there were still psychological problems. There is no doubt that the sensory loss has an effect on the behaviour of the deaf individual – in children, the deaf are often noted to be emotionally withdrawn and to show frequent compulsive traits or rituals that are performed over and over again. When I started at St Helen's, and my handicap became apparent to me, I began to go through obsessive rituals, day in day out. My cuddly toys and bears had to be 'just so' on the bed and were constantly rearranged according to the day of the week. Every morning and evening I would greet them each individually, give them a kiss and place them in their respective positions. And I always had to make sure that I touched their resting place with my left hand before putting them down on it with my right hand. Getting dressed was an extremely slow process, for I would put my clothes on in a certain order which never changed. I even did my buttons up in a special way. Then I would walk around my room touching every piece of furniture, so that not one stick of furniture 'would feel left out' while I was away from home each day at school. I got to the point where I ate my meals in a certain way – vegetables first, then meat last of all (even to this day I sometimes find myself unconsciously eating meals exactly like this!). I carried out these rituals, and many others, obsessively, always fearing that something would go wrong if I didn't. It gave me a sense of security and firmness, but it drove my mother mad!

This emotionally withdrawn behaviour can be explained by several theories. It is difficult for the deaf child to make sense of incoming information, and it is an almost impossible task for them to co-ordinate the information into a meaningful whole. This makes the deaf child unsure of himself, and others begin to avoid him. Sometimes deaf children feel rejected by their contemporaries and think that these ritals will work magic. Deaf children can be over-stimulated, and may withdraw into a familiar world of their own creation which they know well. Of course, all these forms of behavioural problems can occur in any child, whether he is handicapped or not, but if one imagines a situation where visual stimulus is being used to try to communicate with the deaf child, who may well be experiencing partial or distorted hearing, all this combines to form a confusing barrage – like trying to concentrate on several flashing lights at once – and can lead to stress. Hence the often noted 'tantrum syndrome', which is so typical of the deaf child, can often be regarded as a defence mechanism, or 'displacement activity', to prevent the deaf child becoming over-aroused.

Deafness can lead to learning difficulties, even subnormality, so that the deaf child has two handicaps to cope with. The deaf child has fewer experiences to draw on, and learning by imitation is often impossible. He may remain physically dependent for longer than is normal, may be emotionally immature – for after all, he must resort to means of communication relied on by younger children, like crying and shouting. And the attitudes of those around him may retard his general development, for it is difficult to treat a physically handicapped, limited child in the same way as a normal child of the same age. He may be shielded from contact with other people. This happened to me. Always a teacher would have to step in and stop the other girls from bullying me. It got to the stage where I would often only play near to a teacher, because I was actively discouraged to stick up for myself. I was always told to 'leave it to the teacher to handle', and treated as if I was helpless. I was in serious danger at one time of developing a further problem through boredom and frustration at my inability to fend for myself – and that would have been a secondary handicap I could well do without.

My mother had not wanted to see me grow up miserable and frustrated and so had insisted on me being sent to a normal hearing school, and not to a special school for the deaf where I would then be segregated with my own handicap group from an early age. Arguments that my mother put forward for me to attend a normal school included the point that any deaf child would at some stage have to come to terms with the normal world. So she argued that it was better to keep me in that world, and not isolate me with my own handicap group. And the integration of deaf with normal children would familiarise all with the problems of dealing with handicaps. It worked at Miss Maycock's, where children had known me before I went deaf and were at a more adaptable age. But the theory did *not* work at St Helen's, where the children were at an age when anything unusual immediately became a target for abuse. A deaf child in a normal school may be isolated and rejected by his contemporaries on account of his physical disability. The deaf child is affected by other people's behaviour – whether it is their willingness to understand the problem and help, or to reject him and his problems. I naturally missed out since deafness is beyond any doubt one of the most isolating handicaps there is. It is like being inside a glass box. Even when in close proximity with all the people in my class, I felt mentally light years apart. I was to a large extent dependent on another person's services – usually Clare or my teacher. I relied on their patience and understanding. I needed whatever help could be given in order to enable me to join in as much as possible. But I couldn't always rely on help being given and so a certain amount of ridicule and misunderstanding occurred. This did nothing for my self-confidence, and my inferiority complex grew as I felt more and more inadequate and frustrated at being unable to cope.

It may sound as if I am hammering my own age group and blaming them for everything that went wrong during these years from 1971 to '73. But I'm not using them as a scapegoat or as an excuse for the fact I was unhappy. I'm the first to admit that my character is far from perfect. I was perhaps too insistent that I should be treated 'normally' – which in many ways was absurd because there were so many ways in which I had to have 'special' treatment. I always had to sit in the front of the class. I had to hold the teacher's hand when crossing the road as I couldn't hear the cars coming. I suppose I fought too hard to be 'normal' and tried to ignore my handicap instead of accepting it. It must have been difficult for the other girls to know how to react to me if I didn't freely admit that I needed help. Even worse, I frequently denied needing help which I often *did* require.

I subconsciously knew that I was 'less able' than they were, and so I had an obsessive desire to be better than they in other ways in order to compensate. This was the birth of an extremely difficult, obstinate, stubborn, aggressive and competitive streak that was to continue until my early teens. It must have been difficult for the other girls to understand me, as I was often too persistent and determined in areas where they were more than prepared to let go. Deaf people often tackle 'the problem' with an excess of zeal. They often push themselves too hard and try to fill roles which they are in fact incapable of performing efficiently.

A deaf person with a self-perception radically different from the way others see him is likely to be maladjusted. The better adjusted have positive self-perceptions and plenty of self-esteem. They are less aggressive and less anxious than the poorly adjusted. They are less likely to be annoyed or upset by what they feel is unfair treatment or tactless behaviour. They are also better able to tolerate uncertain, ambiguous or even embarrassing situations when they are unsure of how others will react to them. They have less need of social approval and are better able to rely on their own judgements – particularly about their own performance. These things affect the deaf person's circle of friends and family: they begin to relate his achievements and character to him as an individual rather than to his condition. I've no doubt that at St Helen's I was maladjusted and far too aggressive for my contemporaries to be able to cope with.

Ignorance, however, prevented them from realising why I often behaved so badly and they were too young to understand the implications of deafness as a handicap. All they did realise was that it made me different and hard to get to know. So many of them couldn't be bothered with me. Perhaps, if I had been a bit more passive, they would have taken me under their wing. But, on the other hand, if I had been less determined, I should probably never have mastered accurate speech and never have got to where I am today. Yet I had to learn the hard way. A deaf person confronting the hearing world has to go through a lot of 'aggro' before a mutual understanding is reached.

My years at St Helen's were not without gain, for it was there and then that I finally accepted the need to wear headphones in class. In many cases, headphones or hearing aid can be a third handicap to the deaf child, making him self-conscious and impairing his recognition of his handicap. They are bad for self-confidence. I had only just resigned myself to wearing my hearing aid after months of struggling with my mother, but I still resented having to wear a radio-headphones-type aid in class. It was so conspicuous. Nobody would fail to notice those big clumsy earphones on my head. The microphone the teacher wore round her neck was plain for all to see. And there were two big boxes, one on my desk, one on the teacher's, which completed the apparatus.

I used to moan about this continually to Clare. How could I possibly be normal, I protested, with a pile of junk like that on my desk? She just used to listen quitely until one day she dropped a bombshell.

'You know, Jessica,' she said very straightforwardly, 'you might not like to catch me saying this, but I envy you wearing those headphones.'

I stared at her aghast and clenched my teeth. This sounded like treachery, coming from a friend.

'True, honestly,' she said, 'I do. You look so important in them – just like one of those astronauts you see on the TV, you know. I really envy you.'

I was dumbfounded. The idea had never occurred to me before. 'Really?' I asked cautiously. 'What do the others in the class think?'

'Oh, same as me,' she continued casually. 'But we didn't

want to upset you by telling you as we know you detest wearing them so much.'

'What?' I stammered. 'You envy me wearing them?'

'Sure,' she said and, casual as ever, changed the subject.

Now I saw my headphones in a different light. From then on, my headphones and I were inseparable. I looked forward to wearing them every lesson and relished every moment of the times I was able to wear them. Such a drastic change brought a marked response from my teachers. They could not understand why there were no further tears and 'tantrum syndromes' every time it was cautiously suggested that I should put on my headphones. They could not comprehend the change which had come over me – I believe some of them even got worried in case I was ill! The thing was, that beforehand I had been ashamed to wear them because I felt a fool. I thought the others in the class were laughing at me or looking down on me. Once I realised there was nothing to be ashamed about at all, I became less self-conscious about them. They eventually became like the pair of glasses the teacher often wore – forgotten until somebody mentioned them. What was more – I didn't just wear them, I used them to their maximum advantage to exploit what little residual hearing I still retained. Put it this way: an aircraft is a superb piece of engineering, but useless without a trained pilot at the controls. My hearing aid really had been 'a pile of junk' – as I had dismissively called it – until I became willing to operate it constructively.

One hurdle in my life had been got over – much to my parents' relief!

Around this time, I also began to be taken out of class for peripatetic teaching. A trained teacher of the deaf would visit the school once a week and have a private session with me on my own in order to discuss problems or go over work. This may sound a good idea in theory, but in practice I simply baulked.

From my point of view, it meant a great deal of unnecessary embarrassment. The headmistress would enter our formroom. Everybody would scramble to their feet and say, 'Good morning' in chorus. The lesson would be interrupted and the headmistress would beckon me out of the room, announcing, 'The Speech Therapist is here'. All I was aware of was a feeling of being acutely different from everyone else and I used to feel really shy and awkward as I put my pencil down, took off my headphones (which then whistled loudly owing to electronic feedback before being switched off at the wall), grimaced at the disruption, coloured as more attention was focused on me, and stumbled towards the door, feeling my classmates' steady gaze on my back.

I would reach the empty classroom where the speech therapist would be waiting, complete with uncomfortable headphones. He would exchange a few awkward polite words with my headmistress, who would then leave us. Only then began the long ritual which repeated itself with unfailing tedium each time. I would be made to pronounce my 'difficult' words properly – I hated this – and then we would go over my work. I deplored the whole business. All the time, my poor peripatetic teacher, who was in fact an extremely nice man, was struggling to teach me, while all I wanted was to be back in the classroom being 'normal' again. It is for this reason that I feel a deaf child ought to be able to have his peripatetic teaching *at home*. This way, the process may be more comfortable, partly because the environment is more relaxed, with the added security of knowing that mother is in the kitchen, only yards away. Also, the child feels far less self-conscious and no unwanted attentions are drawn to the handicap. The child isn't made to feel embarrassed, awkward and different in front of the whole class. Work can proceed without inhibition.

There is no doubt that it is easier for the school teachers to keep the peripatetic informed about the pupil's special needs if the extra classes are held at school. But surely other methods of communication could be used and the necessary information got across by letter or 'phone.

What I hated most about being taken out of lessons was that when I came back I had missed a good half-hour's work. My schoolwork suffered a great deal from these frequent interruptions and I often found myself having to try to catch up.

I remember how I used to try and avoid these lessons. I would hide in the playground so that the staff would have to come and look for me. I would go to the loo after the headmistress had gone and would take ten times longer than usual over it.

There was even one occasion when the night before my peripatetic lesson was due I ate half a pound of cheddar washed down with a great deal of Ribena. I was so sick during the night that school next day was out of the question. The pleasure of escaping my peripatetic lesson made all the vomiting worth while.

CHAPTER SEVEN

To Primary School

I left St Helens sooner than I thought I would. It all came about one morning when Mum and Dad called us into their bedroom because they had 'something nice to tell us'. The 'something' turned out to be that 'Dad had a new job as Headmaster of a school in Surrey called Charterhouse' and 'that it was all very exciting and we were moving in August'.

The connections which my mother had with Charterhouse were many. When she was younger her father, Sir Robert Birley, had been Headmaster there and she had spent most of the early period of the Second World War there when she was only ten years old. She was returning now as the headmaster's wife.

Later I found that our links went even further back. My maternal grandmother's father, Eustace Frere, was an extremely able architect, who in his latter years had taken on the job of looking after the London Charterhouse. He renovated and updated the place and, in spite of the fact that the school had long since moved to Godalming, links with the London Charterhouse continued to be strong. My grandmother had moved into the London Charterhouse at the tender age of six weeks and had remained there until her marriage to Robert Birley in the 1920s. Charterhouse was, therefore, a very strong, even dominant thread in the tapestry of our family history.

I was eager to get to school and tell everybody the news, but once the initial novelty of the coming move had worn off I completely forgot about it. I don't remember the actual move itself being a very great upheaval at all. While it was in progress, my sisters and I went to stay with Katherine (the nurse who used to work for our family and who finally succeeded in getting me to drink my milk when I was in hospital) and her family, who had a cosy little house in Windsor. We enjoyed ourselves tremendously and when it was time to go to our new home we were not over-keen to leave. What I remember most about those few days are the games we played in the Great Park of Windsor and the visits we made to the Safari Zoo there. My sisters were terrified of the lions and adored the dolphins. For me it was the other way round. It was the lions, tigers and the shark which attracted my attention, and I squealed with delight when the baboons attacked our car. I thought the dolphins wet and a bit sloppy – they did not interest me much. It was the middle of August and we had lovely weather and I don't remember feeling at all sad or disturbed by being uprooted from the home I had known since I was two. I am aware that moving house may have a profound effect on some deaf children, however. For them, it may at first be difficult to comprehend what is happening. Then they will have to begin all over again, making friends in a new area and this may add to their insecurity. These problems can befall any child, but are highlighted by a handicap such as deafness.

One of the immediate effects of the move was that I had to change schools. Camilla was not due to start at the kindergarten until after Christmas but Natasha and I began straight away at St Mary's in Shackleford, which was a primary school for boys and girls up to the age of eleven.

When I first arrived at St Mary's I was introduced to the class by the lady teacher of the kindergarten who was acting headmistress for the term. She took me in and said something along the lines of: 'This is Jessica who has come to be with us. Now you must all be very nice to Jessica – she's very special. She's deaf and can't hear so you must all face her when you speak and speak clearly because she needs to lipread you. But she is *no different* from you in *any other way*, so please let's all make her feel at home'. There was a big 'AAHHH' issued by all the class and they all said hullo in chorus.

I know of many deaf people who would be extremely offended by this sort of introduction and would consider it condescension of the highest order. They may even go so far as to say that it immediately makes them different from, and inferior to, everybody else on the grounds that it sets them apart and outlines their disability. They claim that since the other people are now aware of the disability, they feel embarrassed to talk to the deaf person.

I disagree totally.

It is unfair on a large group of people if you suddenly enter their lives and expect them to treat you like anyone else when you *need* special attention – if, for example, you need it for them to make the effort of looking at you whilst speaking and to speak more slowly into the bargain. If the group do not know of the problem and the deaf person, finding it too difficult to cope, then breaks down and bursts into tears, the group will probably feel guilty even though it was not their fault since they had no idea of the deaf person's handicap. Even worse is the situation where the deaf person gets angry with the hearing people and accuses them of being uncaring or selfish when in fact the hearing people were unaware of the deaf nature of the individual. All it needs is a simple explanation from the deaf counterpart, and a bit of imagination on behalf of the hearing people. It is best to specify the problem right from the start and to be completely frank about it. The deaf must help hearing people to understand the complex difficulties of deafness. Only then can they expect a sympathetic response. After all, how can one expect one's contemporaries to help if the latter do not know how to? Simple requests like 'Please turn the light on so I can see to lipread you' are not usually troublesome to either party. It is also important to appreciate any efforts they make on behalf of you (the deaf person) and not to take it for granted. There are a great many disabled people who automatically expect other people to bend over backwards for them (without providing any explanation of the problem involved). And they get decidedly annoyed when the opposite occurs. They then blame non-handicapped people unfairly.

I feel this sort of handicapped peevishness is all a bit futile. From my experience, people have always been willing to help once the problem has been clearly explained. I am deaf enough to need people to face me while speaking and I am not going to ignore my handicap in the hope that it will go away – why not? Because it won't. And the more you ignore it, the worse the psychological effects will become.

Some people do choose to ignore their handicap altogether,

S.S.S.-C

and I feel this is a mistake. An important element in a person's self-concept is his perception of the roles he can play towards others and his perception of the roles they want to play towards him. He needs to adjust to his handicap and realise exactly what his difficulties are. It may be that in the case of some people who are fortunate enough to have *some* hearing (i.e. if their deafness is not severe) they will have no *need* to disclose their handicap if they feel they will injure their pride by doing so. They may be depressed or even horrified by the fact that they are expected to be part of a handicapped group and will avoid all association with deafness. All I can say is 'Good luck to them'. But if deafness, as a problem, is tackled logically, pragmatically in a reasonable determined manner, the problem seems greatly diminished.

It *is* true that some hearing people would feel embarrassed by a person's deafness if they knew it existed. Indeed I have been in many situations when finding myself unable to lipread after two attempts, I have explained politely that I am deaf. I have asked them to please speak a bit more clearly, only to be greeted by embarrassed stares, mumble, awkward apologies or even hasty departures (although, fortunately, these have been rare). But if a hearing person knows that a person is deaf and feels embarrassed it is probably due to ignorance more than anything else. Hence it is up to the deaf person to remedy the situation and put the hearing person at ease.

Many hearing people, through pure ignorance, associate deafness with senility or mental handicap and assume that any deaf people they meet will not be mentally 'all there'. If the deaf person involved is unfortunate enough also to possess bad unintelligible speech this only serves to reinforce the hearing person's misconception.

There was an article in *The Times* in February 1976 which stated that a coach full of fifty or so deaf children returning from London was involved in a multiple motorway collision. Fifteen of the children and the hearing supervisors were badly hurt. Doctors at the hospital had difficulty in identifying and treating the children because of their disabilities. Some doctors, not realizing at first that the children were deaf, thought that they were silent or unintelligible through shock. The Police had to find members of a local church for the deaf at an evening service and take them to the hospital to communicate with the children.

These children were no less intellectually advanced than their hearing contemporaries – in fact their level of intelligence was close to the average for the nations' children. The crux of the issue is the sordid reality of these frightened, injured children being unable to communicate with the medical staff at the hospital and vice versa. It highlights the educational and social problems which deaf people have. This is a bit hard on the deaf person who then does not only have to struggle to make himself understood, but also to make the other 'normal' person aware of the fact that, although deaf, mentally he is perfectly all right.

I recall that once I was in a bank and I could not lipread the man behind the counter. I told him I was deaf and he immediately began speaking to me very loudly in monosyllables. I stared at him blankly, unable to comprehend what on earth he was doing, and tried to work out this baffling behavioural change towards me. Other customers also turned and stared. He evidently took my blank expression as a sign I *still* could not understand him and grabbing a piece of paper he wrote (and I quote): 'You no understand me? No worry. Me go fetch somebody.'

I was aghast. Looking up at him I said, perhaps a bit too forcefully, 'What the hell are you playing at? Just speak normally like you were doing before – only a bit more clearly and please face *me*.' He immediately looked abashed, apologised profusely and said he had never really met a deaf person before. He was clearly in his forties, a well educated, well dressed, respectable man who really ought to have known better, but you couldn't blame him. It was just total ignorance. As I left the bank I did not feel angry at all – just glad that now one more person would know how to cope next time somebody deaf like me came into the bank.

I think that this is why, when this sort of situation happens, it is up to the deaf person to handle it as tactfully as they can to try and avoid embarrassing the hearing person unnecessarily. The latter probably feels quite guilty enough already. They could even try to turn it into a joke. While waiting at Reading station one day I asked a porter what time the train for Oxford was due.

Since I couldn't lipread his reply I told him I was deaf. He immediately laughed in a somewhat slightly shamefaced manner and mouthed to me without voice, 'Do you want the fast train?'

Quick as a flash I mouthed back at him in the same fashion, 'Yes please – and could you also tell me which platform?'

He was defeated and he knew it, but we both laughed and I got all the information I wanted in a friendly helpful manner. As I left he said, 'That was good for me – thanks!' It really made my day! If I had got angry with him, he probably would have just mumbled something and walked away. I would then have had to go through the whole ritual again with another porter whilst still feeling annoyed with the previous happenings. Also, the first porter would not have been 'educated' – he would have continued to hold the same mental picture of deaf people, but think also that they were inclined to be bad tempered as well. On meeting future deaf people he might not have been helpful to them, either. As it was we both worked the situation out positively, logically between us *and* got a laugh at the same time.

I don't really know why much of the hearing public regard deaf people as 'mentally handicapped'. It could be the look of questioning bewilderment on the deaf person's face. It could be that some hearing people associate deafness with old people who may be also approaching senility – and expect the same pattern in the young deaf. It could be that they are embarrassed by the fact that words completely plain to them (and which most people can understand) are totally incomprehensible all of a sudden to the deaf person. They do not expect anyone to be unable to understand them and are embarrassed when it occurs. They could be put off by the intense manner in which the deaf person watches their lips and facial expressions. The deaf persom may be immobile while lipreading and/or force the person they are lipreading to face them and remain rigid with no natural gesture or movement allowed. This may embarrass the hearing person because it feels unnatural and he may not realise that only 30% of speech sounds are lipreadable. Lipreading is hard work which requires a lot of guessing and working out difficult words from the context of the rest of the sentence. It does not really take much to realise why the look of intense concentration on the deaf person's face exists. But there is no doubt that the deaf person must help the hearing person to come to them first before they can expect any help themselves.

I sympathise, however, with those who have found themselves in situations like these; it is extremely annoying. Not just annoying but embarrassing as well. I have been in several 'Does She Take Sugar?' situations. One that features prominently in my mind occurred when I was taken to hospital once as a semi-emergency and my boyfriend, Marc, came along to keep me company. As soon as the medical secretary in reception heard that I was deaf, she stopped speaking to me and began asking Marc all the questions. She didn't even bother to repeat herself to me, but just assumed that I would be incapable of answering her. I put on my severest manner and asked her to address her questions to me. She was somewhat taken aback. Marc had a hard job keeping a straight face. It's become a funny story, but it was hurtful at the time.

On my first day at St Mary's I found that the teacher's opening speech made the other children immediately aware of my handicap and it made them all want to help me. True, some of them were embarrassed at first, but, since I was a bit of a novelty, curiosity eventually got the better of them and they came over to 'sniff me out'. If only somebody had explained to the class at St Helen's how to help me! (However I don't think it would have worked very well since at that age I was a bit too determined to prove my 'normality' and would have resented an opening speech such as that.)

Quite a few of the children from St Mary's also had parents who worked at Charterhouse. Both Vanessa and Sally had fathers who were housemasters, as did Nicola who later went to Charterhouse with me and proved invaluable in my English lessons where she sat next to me, while Annie's father was the deputy headmaster. We all travelled into school in the morning together and back again in the evenings.

I was the only one who was physically disabled, but there were some children from broken homes or living with divorced parents who were also 'disabled' in a wider sense of the word. There was also a girl there who happened to be the daughter of the class teacher. This was a potential disability in itself which could give rise to a lot of teasing. But I must say Helen seldom, if ever, seemed to have any trouble.

St Mary's was different from any other school I had ever been in before. We did not have a different teacher for each subject, but we had Mrs Forbes all day long, except for French when the form mistress of the form below took over. There was no formal timetable either. We wrote our diaries, did some Maths and some English and then went on to the other subjects such as History, Geography, etc. Sometimes Mrs Forbes would go up to the blackboard and do some Religious Education or Science, but these occasions were comparatively few and far between. Most of the time we worked on our own and went to the teacher if we wanted something such as a new mathematical principle explained. Often she came round to check we were working (and not chatting, as was often the case). Any work we did was immediately marked and pupils worked at their own pace through a series of maths books. This meant the bright ones worked faster and were not held back by the slower ones; the latter also benefited by not being rushed. When a peripatetic teacher did come to the school to see me, Mrs Forbes simply tapped me on the shoulder and told me quietly that Ms Russell was waiting in the room where they stored the council school lunches before giving them to us. I would leave the room with no hassle to return later just as unobtrusively and settle down to work again happily not having missed anything. There was no embarrassment, no fuss, and no bother. No lessons were interrupted and the other children's concentration was not disturbed.

This system of teaching suited me fine. It could be tailored to suit the needs of the individual and this included the other pupils as well. Since I was deaf, reading was very important to me. I loved reading and consciously trying to widen my vocabulary. Mrs Forbes encouraged this and was always ready to explain any difficult words I encountered; I often took off to the little corner in the room which was well stocked with books. She did not stand any nonsense, however: she always made sure enough attention was paid to my other subjects, especially maths, which was my weak spot due to my inability to lipread my former maths teachers. Nothing was neglected but I remember her as always being ready to help me with difficult areas and when I had completed the statutory maths requirement for the day she would allow me to read for about an hour as a 'reward' before doing something else. Hence I worked harder at my maths than I would have done otherwise. The atmosphere was relaxed, friendly and she was easy-going but firm: I don't remember her ever having much trouble from our large class (which could get pretty boisterous at times, thanks to some rather hyper-active males of the species).

We had a lot of outdoor games and physical education and there were opportunities to go swimming. At times we would simply stop and have a singing lesson with teacher on the piano while we sang hymns and folk songs at the top of our voices. Some people who were exceptionally good at singing even had lessons from her as she was musical herself.

I feel that this sort of education is very good for deaf children such as myself since it is very flexible and allows children with specific needs to be attended to. But it *does* need a firm teacher in charge, such as we had, to make sure that the pupils don't just end up doing their favourite subjects all day long: if allowed I would probably have read all day and would not have done any maths. Some people would even try and get away with doing nothing at all. Worse still, some people would be inactive simply because they would have no idea *what* to do. With us, there were certain basic requirements. One *had* to do a certain amount of maths, English, etc., every day, which did not leave much time for one to be idle.

The only thing I did not like about St Mary's was story-telling time. I could not really lipread well enough to follow this at any great length, while many of the words would not be within the boundaries of my vocabulary. I would have to learn them later when teacher went over them with me. Hence story-telling time bored me crazy. At times like these, I would simply slip out of my chair and leave the room quietly to play a little social visit on Camilla who had by now joined the kindergarten. She always seemed pleased to see me at any rate. If I could not be bothered to go and see her, I would simply pick up a book and read or get on quietly with some work: nobody seemed to mind! Apart from this I enjoyed St Mary's thoroughly. It was there that I had my first boyfriend – we thought we were terribly daring to hold hands behind the games shed during break! Sadly that romance only lasted a week!

I became very keen on ballet round about this time and at one time went through the stage that many other little girls go through when they want to grow up to be famous ballerinas. All I wanted to do was dance. I had ballet lessons nearby at a place called the Ann Rogers Broach School for Dancing, and really looked forward to each one every week. Lessons were held in the public library hall and there were lots of pupils. I could just feel the vibrations of the piano and hear the low notes well enough to be able to follow. Most of the time I kept up by watching what the other girls were doing and copying them at the same speed. It seemed to work. Gradually I memorized the speed at which a certain step was executed and I would perform it without watching anyone else – in perfect time to the music, too, much to the amazement of everyone including the teacher! Tricks like these gave me immense satisfaction even if they were a bit sadistic.

Ballet should not be denied to deaf children just because they may not be able to hear the music. If the deaf child has any residual hearing, he or she may be able to pick up the low frequency notes on the piano if they are positioned near enough and are wearing a hearing aid. This is invaluable as it encourages them to use their residual hearing to a greater extent. I admit I sometimes had problems while I was leaping about a lot and my hearing aid would fall out of my ear much to the amusement of the class. But in general my aid helped and I sometimes secured it in place with sticky tape.

Music also presents a new kind of sound to the ears of a deaf person and any experience of new sounds is, of course, extremely important. But music has something else to offer in that it is several types of sound which can be all produced mechanically yet at the same time all be made to blend together in perfect harmony. Hearing children are exposed to this and I don't see why deaf children should be denied the sound of music on account of their handicap. (This is only one of the aims of the Beethoven Fund For Deaf Children – to which I shall return in Chapter 14.)

Ballet is largely the art of moving to music. Hence the deaf child can come to appreciate how ballet makes the bodily movements blend with music harmoniously to create so beautiful a spectacle. Since ballet is also a medium of expression, I found myself better able to translate my feelings into gestures. As a result my bodily as well as facial expressions improved and so I became more co-ordinated and relaxed while speaking. More subtle advantages of having done ballet did not show until later. The way in which one has to hold oneself upright is of vital importance to the art. Shoulders should be back, head held high and the body must be carried well, gracefully and smoothly. This can only be achieved by training, but years later I was grateful for all that rigorous drill at the bar. If I was ever in an embarrassing situation when I walked into a room of people who knew I was deaf but did not quite know how to react to me, I always had the confidence of knowing that at least I could hold myself well and look good and not suddenly fumble around awkwardly or fall over my feet in front of everybody. Comportment is a big factor in confidence – which is vital for handicapped people in social confrontations. You can usually tell by a person's walk whether they are nervous or not; so to be able (after years of training) to look and hold myself in a confident manner and disguise my nervousness. I found that I could put other people at ease more quickly.

As I got older, events such as discos came into their own, and instead of just being a word I occasionally read in magazines, the word 'disco' came to be a reality. At times like these, as I went on to the dance floor, I was always grateful for my ballet training. For a start people would stare at me and I *knew* they were doing so (so did all my friends who danced with me and informed me that so-and-so had pointed to me and was talking to someone else about me). I knew they were all wondering how the hell I was going to be able to dance when I could not hear the music. It would be relief to my mind to know that at least I knew how to move my body rhythmically without any awkward, jerky movements (which would have made me stand out even more).

I knew that I could at least make myself *look* as if I knew what I was doing; I would just let my body sway and I would watch my friends to make sure I kept up with the beat and did not fall behind or go too fast. Gradually people would stop looking at me, and having passed the first hurdle, I would then really let myself go. I felt 'normal' and this gave me a psychological lift. If I had not known what to do with my body in response to music in the first place, I would probably have given up without even trying. I might have consequently missed the common teenage experience of disco-dancing, and since this is one way of meeting the opposite sex, I would have lost a lot. I eventually enjoyed ballet and any other forms of dancing (such as disco or tap dancing) so much that I went on to take several exams and passed them. I was especially proud later on, while at Tormead School where I also had lessons given by a visiting teacher. In a large class of hearing girls, only two of us passed a very stiff final exam. For this I got the ballet cup at the end of term which I went up on to the stage to collect while everybody cheered and clapped. It was put amongst the house cup collection and for days afterwards my family got sick and tired of me bragging. My mother was very proud of the fact, but I don't think Camilla benefited so much! She once came home from school and complained to me with frenzied gestures, 'The ballet teacher thinks that just because *you* were good I ought to be a budding Fonteyn! So when I simply *can't* do it, she says "Jessica was good – what's wrong with you?" '

And I must say she certainly did sound pretty fed up!

CHAPTER EIGHT

Earless in Guildford

I was only at this little village school in Shackleford for a year, however, and when I left I went to Tormead School for Girls in Guildford. Natasha and Camilla were there with me. Fortunately they were in the junior school which was housed in a separate building across the road from the middle school where I was.

Sometimes the siblings of the deaf child suffer a lot from having a deaf brother or sister in their midst. Some of them feel neglected by comparison and come to resent all the extra time which the parents often have to spend with handicapped children in order to enable them to live as full and normal a life as possible. Obviously this must not be allowed to happen and I was lucky that my mother handled the situation so well that there was little if any jealousy. Everyone was encouraged to correct my mispronunciation of words – it was not just left to the parents. I feel this is important as long as the other children can say the words properly too. A deaf child presents a responsibility to a family and it is the whole family who must unite and act together if the deaf child is to be helped fully. The worst thing that can happen is when the deaf child's education is left solely to the mother so that the two become segregated from the rest of the family. The acceptance of a deaf child is a problem which the entire family must overcome since the natural pattern of social interactions may be violently disturbed.

Sometimes siblings may be embarrassed by the deaf child in the family and his (probable) immature behaviour. They hence become reluctant to bring friends home as they find it difficult to explain their deaf brother or sister to their friends. They may also feel a sense of guilt – that they do not help the deaf child enough by explaining TV programmes to him or by integrating him into their own circle of friends. Often they tend to feel the deaf child is spoilt on account of the handicap. Yet the siblings' reactions are often a reflection of the way the parents themselves react to and handle the situation. In my family, friction of this sort rarely occurred because I was made to do menial tasks such as clearing away, washing up, laying the table and tidying up my own bedroom just like everyone else. If I misbehaved, as was often the case, I was not excused punishment but was treated like the other members of the family. In fact, if anything, my mother was stricter with me than with my brothers and sisters because a spoilt deaf child is worse than a spoilt hearing child. I was pulled up for every example of bad behaviour and never allowed to get away with it on account of my deafness. A favourite trick of mine was sometimes to turn my head away or walk off in the other direction when my mother asked for help with the washing up. In other words, I went 'very deaf' indeed, and would not turn round when summoned. If my mother ever caught me doing this she excused the others and more often than not I found myself doing the task all on my own. This took ages and I hated it. I soon learned pretty quickly not to use my deafness as an excuse.

I must have exasperated Natasha at times, though, because I relied on her a lot to explain to me what someone was saying when I couldn't lipread them. This was partly unfair on her since she had a moral obligation to help me: she couldn't just tell me to clear off because she knew perfectly well my deafness was not my fault. Yet this did not stop the whole thing being a strain on her since I relied much more on her than any of my other brothers and sisters. I knew too that I exhausted her patience sometimes. This made things doubly difficult for her because she had to help me knowing I resented the dependence inflicted by my handicap.

Recently she recalled to me that while I was taking the entrance exam to Mary Hare Grammar School (residential) for the deaf, I had said to her, 'I want to go away to boarding school because then you'll look forward to me coming home instead of being fed up with me all the time.' I really hated not being able to be as independent as I would like to have been. I hated always having to have TV programmes explained to me, but it was better than not being able to understand anything at all; having to have somebody telephone for me instead of being able to do it myself; having to sometimes use my sister as an intermediary-cum-interpreter if I myself could not lipread someone, and a hundred and one other irritating little things. Sometimes I took it for granted she would always help me and accuse her of being impatient or lazy if she didn't appear over-helpful. It was not until Christmas 1979/80 that I fully realised the effect a deaf person can have on brothers and sisters if matters are left to go too far.

We were in Gstaad ski-ing at the time, having spent Christmas out there. My mother had by this time been dead about a year and I had just automatically shifted all the responsibility for supplementing my lipreading onto Natasha's shoulders without giving the matter much thought. Now she was always expected to tell me 'what everyone else was talking about,' etc. It almost became a twenty-four hour job for her whenever I was at home. Yet because my mother had always seemed able to cope with it, I just assumed Natasha would too, without taking into account the fact that she was not as old, experienced or mature as mother had been. So what before had been a bit difficult for her now became totally unbearable.

We went out to dinner with another family and I got thoroughly miserable because I was seated far away from Natasha and I simply could *not* follow the conversation as it darted swiftly from lip to lip. I was truly 'isolated in a crowd'. Everybody else seemed to be engaged in interesting conversation except myself, and it was infuriating when they suddenly all fell about laughing when I had no idea what the joke was even about. There were few ways I could join in spontaneously since I did not even have a clue about the lines upon which the subject matter was progressing. To cut a long story short, my frustration at my handicap reached a peak. I sat there fuming until it was time to go home, which seemed like hours. Once home, I snapped at Natasha and went to bed. Poor Tash – she hadn't a clue what to do.

When it was announced we were going to dinner with the same family again a few days later, I nearly threw a fit. While getting ready in our bedroom I suddenly burst into tears and said that I wasn't going and that 'wild horses wouldn't drag me there'. Natasha asked why: and this was just too much for me. I yelled at her that she didn't know what it was like to be deaf, that she had no idea of my handicap and that I hated her for it – in fact I hated the whole world for it. How would she like it if she was as isolated as I was? Then I started telling her that she did not do nearly enough to help me and that she was lazy and I hoped very much her conscience was as guilty as hell. When I looked at her after this great tirade I noticed she was crying as well. Just to show how inconsiderate I was towards her I immediately assumed that she was upset because she felt sorry for me and that she 'realised' she was not helping me enough – that my speech had aroused her pity to such a profound extent. Half expectantly, half contemptuously I said, 'Well then?' waiting for her to apologise profusely and tell me she now understood my deafness better and would help me more.

I was totally unprepared when she raised her head and yelled back at me, 'It's bloody hard for me as well you know!'

Those words really shook me. I had never thought of it that way before. She then carried on, telling me about how little I seemed to appreciate it when she put herself out for me – rarely did I say 'thank you' or even 'please' in the first place for that matter. If she missed part of a TV programme while explaining the previous happenings to me, nobody explained what she had missed to her. This was absolutely true: in fact, all of what she was saying was absolutely true. She pointed out that if she ever refused to explain something to me, not only I but the rest of the family chided her. There were many other things she said: that I expected her to help me on the 'phone and to help me immediately even if it was the middle of *Top of the Pops* or if she was in the process of working out a complex mathematical problem which she could ill afford to leave. If I was unable to lipread someone at a cocktail party, for example, I would immediately grab her and expect her to interpret on the spot without caring if she was having an interesting conversation with someone else. I would just interrupt and embarrass her by not even giving her time to excuse herself. Yet she could not refuse to help me in front of everyone or even tell me to wait because that would also be rude. Everything she said was totally justified criticism and for perhaps the first time I saw that I really was expecting too much of her. I felt really ashamed and still do sometimes now when I look back on it.

Things got much better almost immediately. I stopped relying totally on her but also asked other members of my family what was happening on TV. This took some getting used to because they had rarely done it before so they were not as experienced as Tash and not able to do it as quickly. Sometimes the temptation to resort to asking her alone was very strong but I managed to resist it, knowing it would only serve to make matters worse if I didn't. Whenever I needed help on the 'phone, I asked more politely and waited until she was free to do so. Furthermore I thanked her afterwards – maybe not always verbally: a hug, a kiss, or a wink will usually do. But I did not take it for granted any more.

When in a situation where I could not understand what someone was saying to me, I first tried harder to understand. If this did not work, I explained I was going to get Natasha, or someone else who happened to be nearby. I would give Natasha the signal but not in such a demanding manner and I would wait for her at least to excuse herself.

I'm not saying life was suddenly a bed of roses for both of us. There were still days when I shouted at her or when she felt tired and did not appear over-eager to help. But on her part she tried to understand better how difficult it could be for me while, before, she had resented me too much to make much effort in that area. We got on much better after that now a mutual understanding was reached and our respect for each other was greater.

Yet this treatment of her mainly stemmed from jealousy even though I was, for the most part, unaware of it. There is a tendency for deaf people to regard 'non-deaf' people as being 'perfect' and this breeds envy to a profound extent. Deaf people often feel that hearing people are better off because they are not so easily isolated and are more readily and naturally integrated into a social group.

While we were at Tormead, however, and while my mother was alive, my deafness did not affect my sisters all that much except for Natasha having to help me when we were at home in cases where my mother was not immediately available. There were perhaps a few times when other children asked them what was wrong with my ears and they had to explain. Camilla once told a friend of hers very pointedly, 'Well, you see, it's like this: they just don't work.' Camilla could be quite blunt and to the point when she wanted to be. Once she came home from school calmly announcing that her best friend was no longer speaking to her but that she didn't really care. Philip asked her why and she just as candidly reported that it was due to the fact she had told her friend that the latter's brother was 'as weak as a squashed ant'. When the friend had told her to take the remark back, Camilla had replied 'Oh, but I meant it'. I've always wondered how she has managed to live so long.

Sometimes my brothers and sisters may have been made to feel a bit small if a teacher or someone praised my performance as a deaf child in a hearing school. Many years after I left Tormead, Camilla was in an English class with my former English teacher. The teacher was criticising the form's performance in a dictation set recently and one girl put up her hand and said the reason for her having made so many mistakes was because she had unable to hear the teacher. The teacher reprimanded her sharply saying that 'Jessica Rees who was an extremely deaf girl' had been in her class and had 'always coped with dictation perfectly well'. This was embarrassing for Camilla.

But it was a great compliment to me that neither Natasha nor Camilla introduced me to their friends as being 'my deaf sister'. I was simply 'My eldest sister . . . and by the way look at her when you talk to her' without saying why. This meant they accepted me as being 'normal' and thought of me as a sister who, by the way, happened not to hear very well, instead of as a 'deaf sister'.

I was only at Tormead for one academic year and during that time I managed to get into plenty of scrapes including one episode where I bit the hand of the gym teacher. We were playing on the climbing frame and I fell off. She came over to see if I was all right but I did not want anyone to fuss and refused to let her touch me. In trying to force me to look at her with my eyes open so I could lipread her, she got her hand in the way of my mouth and I didn't bother to stop my teeth from sinking into her flesh. I was severely reprimanded.

There was also an occasion when my maths teacher was absent so I had to go and have my maths lesson that day with another group and the teacher there – unknown to me – did not know I was deaf. I entered late and since there were no seats available at the front, I sat at the back. The sun was in my eyes and I could not see to lipread the teacher talking by the blackboard nor could I make out what was being written. 'Not to worry,' I thought to myself and waited for the teacher to finish so that I could ask her to explain when she came round. In the meantime, I amused myself looking at the pictures on the wall at the other side of the room away from the sun and tracing the cracks on the ceiling.

Finally the teacher came round and as she passed my desk, I stopped her and asked her what she had been saying. She looked very annoyed, which surprised me, and glared at me like nobody's business. Then she announced sarcastically to the rest of the class: 'Here is a girl who is extremely rude. She lounges in her chair and does not even bother to listen to me while I am teaching, but expects individual attention to make up for the time she wastes dreaming. Well, madam,' she said turning to me, 'I'm certainly not going to bother with you!' These last few words were said rather more forcefully than the rest.

I had been assuming she knew all about my deafness. I was aghast. Without thinking I blurted out at her, 'Oh for God's sake, I can't, it's not my fault!'

'Out!' she commanded, 'Get out of my class. I will not have any pupil speaking to me like that.'

I stumbled out of the room tripping over my briefcase on the way. Meanwhile a girl at the back piped up, 'Miss, don't you know she's deaf?' As I closed the door, I felt it being opened again, I turned and found myself face to face with the same teacher who had kicked me out. But there was a different expression on her face. She was crying. She put her arms round me and hugged and told me how sorry she was – she simply had not known about my deafness. This was a bit too much for me, and all of my ten years of age, to suddenly find a teacher who had confused me by being angry with me for no apparent reason, now suddenly crying on my shoulders with remorse. I burst into tears myself and we cried together for a few moments, while the rest of the class calmly looked on. I think most of them were at least a bit moved, and we all agreed later that it was a very generous gesture on her behalf to have shown how sorry she was when she needn't have. Come to think of it, she could have called me back and publicly admonished me for not letting her know I was deaf at the start of the lesson. But she showed she cared and apologised in front of everyone without trying to cover up for her actions, which I think was a very big thing to do. We were all very impressed. 'Sorry' is always a hard word to say.

That episode showed me how rude and arrogant some deaf people may appear to hearing people who are unaware the handicap exists. It also showed me what an awful shock it must be for those people who condemn the deaf person for being rude or arrogant only to find themselves in the 'wrong' when they learn that the person concerned has a hearing handicap.

Apart from this, my time at Tormead was pretty uneventful except for when I surprised everybody, including myself, by winning the ballet cup. My school reports stated that I tried hard but that I found it difficult. It was true. I was always struggling to keep up in subjects where I could not lipread the teachers very well, despite my sitting at the front of the class. English was no problem: I could lipread the teacher perfectly. She knew this and once confessed to me that a former pupil of hers and told her she had a 'big wiggly mouth'. This said it all. She spoke clearly with plenty of facial animation but best of all she did not wave her arms around a lot the way some of the other teachers did. I was exceedingly glad of this – waving one's arms around makes it difficult for the deaf person to see the speaker's mouth clearly hence lipreading is made even harder. She taught me all I then knew about English grammar and she had lots of 'fun' methods of helping the pupils to remember the many grammatical rules. The best known one was the BIC biro rule. B.I.C. stood for Begin with Inverted comma and Capital letter whenever introducing direct speech. You only had to glance at the BIC biro you were writing with to remember it. She also said she would draw a huge red line across the entire page and work with her red BIC biro if anybody got it wrong!

One day all this changed when I went on a routine visit to the Ear, Nose and Throat clinic. There I saw the NHS doctor responsible for the education in the Surrey area of deaf children such as myself.

CHAPTER NINE

We Confront the 'Deaf' Doctor

Far from being a bright sunny morning when 'it all happened' just like one reads about in slushy novels, it poured with rain non-stop and I was in a foul mood.

We had to wait nearly an hour past the appointment time before I was even given an audiometric test. So my mother was not exactly in the best frame of mind either by the time we were finally admitted to the doctor's surgery.

Whenever I went to the doctor I usually just sat there for the most part in silence, while my mother and the doctor talked animatedly. Sometimes the doctor would cross over to where I sat and look into my ears with his instrument and continue talking to my mother whilst doing so. I hated to be talked about as if I was not there, but there didn't seem to be much I could do about it. This time, however, was different. The doctor suggested all of a sudden that I should be transferred to a special school for the deaf, since it was obvious I was having to struggle in order to keep up in hearing schools.

My mother was outraged, and I remember her replying angrily when the doctor asked me how I felt, 'Two years at St Helen's, one year at St Mary's, one year at Tormead and then another change – she'll be a jumping jackpot.'

Her opinion of special schools for the deaf was rather low owing to her own ignorance of them – she had never looked at one in detail or made any attempt to find out about them either. Having always fought to keep me in the hearing world she had no wish to segregate me now with my handicap group alone. Her idea of schools for the deaf was that everyone spoke entirely in sign language. Having worked so hard to get my speech to the level it was and maintaining it there, the last thing she wished was for me to lose it. Not that she had anything against sign language. She agreed it was an efficient alternative or additional mode of communication to speech. But, to her, nothing mattered more than clear speech, so she wanted my speech to remain at least as clear as it was. She knew only too well the usefulness of manual language. When I had first gone deaf she had taught me to speak by using a sort of sign language. It was used to spell out the word I was learning to say or to distinguish by gesture between 'sun' and 'son' which both look and sound the same. Whenever I tried to tell her a word which I was mispronouncing and which she did not grasp, I used to sign it out. This could sometimes be quite amusing. Similarly she would often sign to show me in what context I was to use a new word. But she did not encourage me to sign rather than to speak; in fact she did the exact reverse. My siblings did not sign to me and if I wanted to communicate with them, I was forced to speak and to use my voice properly. Her theory was that if I was only able to sign, I would not bother so much with my speech, because communicating by sign language is much easier. She meant that if I were to walk into a country pub in Devon for example, and make the sign for 'Beer' I would be far less likely to consume any alcohol and end up drunk than if I asked for it by voice! Furthermore, she pointed out, she had been successful at teaching me to speak and lipread from an early age and she did not want this success threatened if I came into contact with people who needed and used a lot of signs.

These were all the arguments my mother flung at the doctor one after the other. I had seldom seen her so annoyed. I remember sitting there playing with the hem of my dress, wondering miserably what the hell all the fuss and shouting was about. The doctor did not give in, however. He pointed out that there were oral schools for the deaf (which did not use sign language) and some very good ones, too. He told my mother that her mental picture of schools for the deaf was old-fashioned and that she would be extremely narrow-minded if she was not prepared at least to consider them as a potential alternative to hearing schools. He said that if I stayed on at hearing schools, I would be lucky to get more than a few CSEs. On the other hand if I went to somewhere like the Mary Hare Grammar School in Berkshire, I would end up just as well qualified as my hearing contemporaries if not better. I was 'not dim' he said, and if something was not done quickly to develop my potential I could end up a frustrated, bored juvenile delinquent.

Before anybody gets angry and says that the doctor had no right to be rude to my mother in that fashion, please allow me to point out that my mother was being jolly rude to him, if not ruder. Furthermore he was only doing his job. He could see what would happen to me if left to swim in an unending whirlpool of frustration which could only get worse as I got older. Indeed, he had actually seen it happen to some children who were as deaf as I was, and whose parents had refused to allow them to move to special schools, but had instead kept them in schools where they were clearly unable to cope. It had become clear to him that prevention was better than cure in the case of deaf children's education. Dr Beet told my mother that my speech was as good as it was ever going to get and agreed that it was 'excellent' and 'near normal'. He pointed out that if I went to an oral school for the deaf it would not get any worse, as there would be trained speech therapists on the staff. He was not concerned about my speech; what he *was* worried about was my level of education which was fast falling below my I.Q. The important thing, he said, was that now that my speech was good, time was long since ripe to concentrate more on my education. If a special school failed to work, there would be nothing to stop my mother from removing me instantly. But it *was* worth a try. He urged my mother to contact the Principal of the Mary Hare even if nothing came of it.

I'm not saying that my mother stormed off in a huff, but she did say goodbye in rather an abrupt fashion. She 'phoned the Principal however, who was exceedingly helpful and invited both my parents to come and visit the school with no obligation. She was later to tell me that it was solely due to the fact he was so rational and polite over the phone that she finally agreed to consider the idea.

I was at school while my parents went to visit the Mary Hare but when I came home in the evening I found that they had both completely changed their former ideas about schools for the deaf. The buildings were beautiful they said, especially the Manor House which served as the girls' residential area and included the administrative offices. It had a large hall area lined with oak panelling, and a huge fireplace. Two common rooms (junior and senior) led off from the hall and both had been well furnished with television, record players, chairs, tables, etc. The school was set in extensive grounds consisting of wooded and open areas. Yet it was only four miles from the nearest town. The main factor which helped my parents make up their minds, however, was the manner in which the children there behaved. They all seemed happy and friendly towards each other. Mum and Dad went into an Art lesson and found the children there quite willing to talk openly about their work and what they were doing. Standards of teaching and speech were seen to be high (even under my mother's ruthless scan). The main objects of the school seemed to be to give the deaf child as good an education as hearing contemporaries had access to: a bright deaf child was not to lose the opportunity of a good education solely because of the handicap. Another aim seemed to be to educate the child to take a rightful place in the hearing world. Speech faults were corrected, however small, and pupils were encouraged to work hard. The teaching staff all seemed interested in what they were doing and willing to give that 'little bit extra'. At the same time my parents noted that the deaf community was by no means segregated from the hearing world. Many deaf girls belonged to the girl guides association in Newbury. Opportunities to go shopping in town were many. There were also several extra-curricular activities such as sailing or woodwork and metalwork on Saturday mornings for those interested.

As far as physical education was concerned, the school was well equipped. There was a lovely swimming pool with glass panes all the way round the outside which gave rise to a bright, sunny swimming area. The football and netball teams often played matches against nearby schools which was seen as another way of integrating hearing and deaf worlds. My parents therefore became quite enthusiastic about the whole scheme. Not having seen the school myself I did not know quite how I should feel, but I agreed to 'give it a go' – mainly for the sake of pleasing my mother.

The entrance examination consisted of two parts. A written

examination was set which over a hundred children completed at their present schools. Round about fifty qualified for an interview, upon the basis of which the final thirty were selected. I thought I did not even stand a chance, so used was I to coming near the bottom in school exams. I did the written exam in a little room next door but one to the headmistress's office and thought no more about it. I did not find it particularly easy nor did I find it particularly hard. But I did like the English paper. We were given a series of pictures almost like a cartoon strip and told to make up a written story to go underneath which fitted with the illustrations. I enjoyed this immensely but that is all I remember of the affair. I quickly forgot all about it, as I did not want to raise my hopes in case I did not pass.

The next few weeks were pretty uneventful until out of the blue news came that I had passed the first round and was expected to attend for interview one day in mid-March. Although I was pleased about it, it was not until my parents decided to celebrate the news that I realised how important the whole project was to them. I was taken out for a meal on my own with both of them. It was the very fact I was taken out alone, with no other member of the family being involved, which really made me aware of how well I had done in their eyes. For once I was not left out of the general mealtime conversation, but my parents talked to ME and nobody else – I got their undivided attention which I thoroughly relished! I was allowed to have exactly what I wanted from the menu, which led to me having melon followed by 'steek and ships' with more melon for pudding. (You may have guessed that the latter ranked high among my favourite foods.)

The day for my interview came. I must confess it was the thought of getting a day off school which appealed to me more than anything else. The drive to Newbury was pleasant enough and my mother and I found ourselves left with an hour or so to spare before having to present ourselves at the school. We decided to drive into the town and see if we could find anywhere to have breakfast. The only place open at such an hour was a pokey little café near the railway station which insisted on serving chips with practically everything (not that I minded much but my mother settled for plain coffee!)

I began to get a bit nervous before we actually entered the school grounds. When we did go through the gates I remember my first reactions being that I thought the place looked even nicer than I had dared to hope. We entered the Manor Hall and a lady with a friendly face approached and asked *me* (not my mother) what my name was. Furthermore she spoke clearly and I had no need to ask her to repeat what she had said. When I replied she glanced down at her list and beckoned to a girl in the school uniform who came forward smiling. She seemed really friendly, the way she said 'hullo' to me and my mother. Then, taking my arm, she led me over to a small table in the corner where my coat was taken off my back and a glass of cold milk thrust into my hand. My mother waved, gave me the thumbs up sign and left. I think she went to have her hair done or something similar to pass the time. I felt a bit lost and alone just then, but not for long. My escort asked me questions about my home and school and chatted on generally to help me warm up. She was ready to tell me all about her school and answer all of my many questions. What struck me most was that she looked at me while speaking *and* spoke clearly. If I ever found it difficult to follow what she was saying, she merely repeated her words slower and surer as if it was the most natural thing in the world to be asked to do. I couldn't quite make it out. Where were all the exasperated looks and gestures of impatience which seemed to be the norm if I ever mentioned the word 'pardon' to my other friends? I noticed the happy, relaxed atmosphere and all of a sudden I desperately wanted to come here and to be one of the crowd to which my escort belonged. I had not known before that it was possible for deaf people to be as well off as they all seemed to be here. My adrenalin began to flow and I was *determined* to pass my interview.

At length after everyone had arrived, we were moved off into a large imposing room with a grandfather clock and white pillars. At this point my escort left me saying she would be back later and wished me luck. It looked out onto a conservatory and beyond the windows one could see green fields rolling away towards the M4. I thought that the room was rather grand and I was somewhat disconcerted to find out later that it was merely the senior girls' common room (and not usually in such a tidy state either!) A tall man with some papers entered and told us to sit down, two to a table, in front of him. He then proceeded to welcome us and started talking about the grandfather clock which he was standing in front of. He was the Principal – and *very* unlike my previous headmistresses. The whole atmosphere he created was much more easygoing. I decided I liked him and I am glad to say that to this day our friendship persists long after I have left the school.

The whole day passed in a blur of I.Q. tests, maths papers, oral examinations, reading aloud tests, comprehension papers and conducted tours of the school by our escorts (which ended, inevitably, in a gorge at the school's tuck shop run by the caretaker's wife with the help of a few pupils). By the end of the day I was even more convinced of my desire to come to Mary Hare. Instead of not wanting to have anything to do with deaf poeple, as had formerly been the case, I suddenly felt proud – not ashamed any more – to belong to a group of people united by one physical disability.

Exposure to people with the same handicap is generally an important experience with a variable effect. To generalise, children tend to find it reassuring that there are other children who have the same problems and that they are not unique. One of the things Mary Hare did for me is that it finally convinced me people wanted to laugh *with* me and not *at* me. I felt relieved to be equal with my contemporaries and as a result much of my earlier aggression evaporated. Gradually I became happy again and less prejudiced against hearing people.

My mother returned to the school to take me home, but before we could leave a teacher stepped in and asked my mother if she minded waiting a while longer because they wanted to do an audiometric test on me. This dismayed me. I got very worried that they might find out how very deaf I was and decide I was too deaf to accept me. Consequently I tried my very best to 'hear' as much as I possibly could, but the shape of the graph on the audiogram did not deviate from the norm at all. I was now convinced that they would fail me and I returned to my mother feeling pretty miserable. The teacher talked with my mother for about half an hour while I played around and chatted to my escorts. I could see the teacher asking questions with raised eyebrows and I began to burn with curiosity. When at last it was all over the teacher rose and shook hands with my mother and me and left us.

I couldn't believe it when my mother told me that they had done the audiometric test to make sure I was really as deaf as I was said to be. The Mary Hare has a policy of accepting extremely deaf border-line candidates in favour of those, also borderline cases, with a higher level of residual hearing. Many people believe the reverse to be true. It is incredible the number of people I have met who hold a grossly misconceived idea that in order to qualify for the Mary Hare the child has not only to be clever but also has to be partially hearing. (Some teachers of the deaf who you would think would know better also hold this wrong idea.) In fact, the deafer you are, the more chance you stand of getting in. The Mary Hare exists to help those with a profound hearing loss, who are unable to cope at hearing schools, to have the chance of a good education which they would otherwise be denied. Borderline candidates who have a lot of hearing are thought to stand a better chance of 'surviving' in a hearing school or a P.H.U (Partially Hearing Unit) attached to a normal school. Hence they are rejected in favour of the deafer border-line candidates who would not be able to cope so well.

The teachers were impressed with the way my mother had taught me to speak and from my speech they had calculated my hearing loss to be not very profound. The audiometric test was a check to make sure I really was profoundly deaf. So in a way I suppose it was a positive sign that they *were* interested in me. The questions my mother had been asked were all about how hard I really was finding it to cope in a hearing school, whether I would benefit from being at Mary Hare, or if I was really O.K. at a hearing school. My mother was also asked about how she had taught me to speak.

It may seem very big-headed of me to thrust my level of speech forward in this way, but in fact I am not asking for any credit for myself. It was all due to my mother and I want everyone to realise what she did for me. In fact I want everyone to realise what parents can potentially do for their deaf child. If any parent were to ask my advice now on what to do for their deaf child, I would say:

(a) Get the deafness diagnosed as early as possible. If the child has any residual hearing get a powerful enough hearing aid and a well fitting earmould immediately after the deafness is diagnosed.

(b) Talk to the deaf child nonstop about anything; use the radio or TV if necessary. Just get the child used to whatever can be heard of the sound of the normal human voice so that he can begin to imitate it.

If the parents are unlucky enough to find themselves with a totally deaf child who has no hearing whatsoever from birth then I fully sympathise, for the child will be deprived of the vital stimuli of the sounds of the human voice. Fortunately such cases are rare. The important thing then would then be to accustom the child to mouth movement associated with gestures in order that lipreading may be started at an early age: for instance 'yes' accompanied by a nod *and* a smile. The child will learn a lot from facial expressions, too. From this, the child can be taught to progress to speech but this would probably need expert supervision.

It was amusing when I found out that I had gained entry to the Mary Hare. The form teacher gave me an envelope to give to my mother but she also seemed very pleased with me for some reason. The envelope bore the school address on the back so I knew the contents held my future. Furthermore the flap was not sealed – just tucked in . . . I was itching to find out whether I had got in, but afraid to open it in case I hadn't. I had a small squabble with Tash as we got into the car to drive home (driven by the mother of a friend of mine) and while we were sulking back to back I suddenly couldn't wait any longer. I slipped the letter out of my pocket and opened the envelope. Tash saw me and said with a shocked expression, 'But Jessica! That letter was for Mummy!' I ignored her, which scandalised her even more, and opened out the letter. The first words I read went along the lines of: 'We are pleased to inform you your daughter Jessica Rees has been accepted for entry to the school in August 1975 and has been placed in form 1R.' It took me a while to work it out because of all the long words and the somewhat formal nature of the letter which I was unused to. When I *did* realise what it meant I was so pleased that I kissed Tash on the spot and our quarrel was instantly forgotten.

'I've got in,' I whispered excitedly.

'Where?' she asked absentmindedly.

'You *know*,' I replied thinking how stupid little sisters could be at times.

She was as pleased as I was but we both agreed we had to greet my mother with a straight face 'as if nothing had happened'. This was difficult since we were so excited, it was difficult to conceal it! Luckily there was small need to look serious and utterly normal because the minute the car entered our drive my Mum came flying out of the house and ran towards us telling us the good news which she had heard earlier that day by telephone.

That night we really let our hair down!

Now I knew I had got in, I got tremendously excited about the whole idea of going away to a boarding school. In fact, when I first went to Mary Hare I was so mischievous that Mr Pearce, the Principal, was heard to remark shrewdly; 'All I can say about Lady Jessica Margaret Ann Rees so far is that she has read a great many books about boarding schools and is determined to make it all happen!'

The best bit was when I went to buy my new school uniform and by doing so got out of another whole day at school! My friends at Tormead were for the most part pleased for me that I had got in, even though one or two were a bit disdainful of the fact that the Mary Hare was a school for the deaf. This didn't worry me – nothing whatsoever could dull my enthusiasm. I couldn't wait for August 19th which was when the first of my annual four terms began at my new school.

CHAPTER TEN

The Special School

Perhaps the first thing I ought to tell you about the Mary Hare Grammar School for the Deaf was that my life was for the most part centred on the manor house I have spoken of previously. The manor was called Arlington Manor and after I had started school there, we discovered that it had once been the home of my great-great-grandmother called Corrie Frere. That is why Corrie is one of our family names. My elder brother has it incorporated into his – Robert Hugh Corrie Rees. It was certainly an incredible coincidence and many of my friends and members of the teaching staff remained sceptical about it for a long while even after I showed them my father's letter as proof.

Perhaps the second thing I ought to explain, in case you are unaware what a difference it makes, is that the Mary Hare is an *oral* school for the deaf. This means that all communication is spoken (or written only in cases of exceptional difficulty) and that sign language is not encouraged. In fact, it is totally barred. To show just how important speech is as opposed to sign language, we had inter-house speech competitions amongst the school's four houses named Arnold, Beverley, Braidwood and Mary Hare – all famous pioneers in deaf education.

There was a large notice-board near the staff room with a long list of all the names of pupils in the school. This was the 'Good Speech Mark' board and every time a teacher heard a pupil speaking very well, or if a pupil tried very hard in a speech lesson, a good mark was awarded to the pupil. The number of good speech marks a pupil possessed could be counted by adding up all the separate initials of teachers after that pupil's name. Next to this board was another identical list of names but this was the 'Bad Speech Mark' board.

A pupil could be awarded a bad speech mark for:

(a) Talking without voice (even if this was only done in

fun or behind a teacher's back in the classroom. It was considered so important to exercise one's voice).

(b) Excessive use of manual sign language (but some natural gesture was allowed).

(c) Not wearing an aid or not bothering to get a broken one repaired.

This last penalty existed because many pupils wore hearing aids to help their speech, that is to say without an aid they would not hear normal human voices and this could lead to a marked deterioration in the quality of their spoken language. Furthermore some pupils could not hear their own voices at all without the use of an aid, so lack of one would in turn lead to loss of the ability to monitor the tone level of one's own voice.

The system worked out quite well. If you scored a good mark for yourself, you also added to the score of your house. If you gained a bad speech mark it counted against yourself and your house. Bad speech marks were rarely given and the sight of one next to one's name could cause a bit of an inner panic. It usually led to a telling-off from the head of house and even the form teacher in some cases. Furthermore, it was there for the whole school to see, which was considered highly undesirable. If anybody collected a larger share of black marks than was acceptable, action was usually taken, although I only remember this happening on one occasion in all of my five years at the school. I got a bad mark once and I remember feeling suitably chastened by it.

There were some drawbacks to this scheme. It was unfair in some ways because there were a few teachers who awarded good speech marks more easily than others. Hence if you had speech teachers who rarely awarded good marks, you would not get as many, however hard you tried, as would your friend who did not have to work so intensely but got several from their more generous speech teachers.

Speech marks were not given indiscriminately but it always seemed to be the pupils with the worst speech who got more marks than anyone else. We accepted this, however, as it was seen as a means of encouraging those with real speech problems to work harder at overcoming them. It was perfectly fair.

Bad speech marks were a problem for some children who had deaf parents who communicated entirely by sign language. These children would be accustomed to sign language as their mother tongue and would often use it automatically, incurring a bad speech mark as they did so. This seemed a bit unfair on them as they had to retain their use of sign language if they were to continue to communicate with their parents while at home. The school held the policy that such children should not sign while in school even outside the formal classroom, but this was easier said than done, and the children concerned had a pretty hard time trying to adjust to the environment they were in each time they changed from school to home and vice-versa.

I can remember once finding one such girl, four forms below me, in floods of tears one Wednesday afternoon. She had just been given yet another bad speech mark. When I asked her what the matter was, she blurted out that she couldn't win either way. I pressed her to clarify what she meant and she said that she *had* to sign to her deaf parents at home and had done so since birth but whenever she was at school she was not allowed to and was given bad speech marks if she did. Yet sign language was her natural mode of communication, it was her mother tongue and she hated being made to feel ashamed of it. She was being made to feel 'Speech good, sign language bad', just as rigidly as the 'Four legs good, two legs bad' motto in *Animal Farm*. Yet she had always been accustomed to thinking 'Speech good, sign language better'.

The real problem came about when she went home at the end of term by which time her use of sign language had lessened. There, her parents would chide her for thinking sign language was 'bad' and make her sign in order to communicate with them. So when the poor girl returned to school at the end of the holidays she would have reverted to fluent sign language and be chided by the teachers and the prefects and given bad speech marks – a seemingly unending vicious circle. I quite agreed with her that it was impossible to win. I am glad to say, however, that as she got older it became easier for her to switch over to sign language or speech depending on where she was and the problem lessened greatly. Also her level of speech improved. This enabled her to communicate fluently with both groups of people. She became bilingual in sign language and speech.

Yet the policy of the school was oralism and only aural-oral communication was acceptable. Great use, however, was made of written language to reinforce spoken language so as to aid mental establishment of the relationships between print-read, lip-read and heard forms, and to emphasise intonational patterns and the syllabic stress which is available to the hearing child automatically.

Hence all sign language had to be abolished and speech had to be the only mode of communication. Not even a marginal amount of sign language could be allowed and no exceptions from the oral rule could be made at all, not even for pupils such as those who had deaf parents. There was one firm rule for everybody which it was easier for some pupils to keep than others.

This may seem unreasonable but the school's argument was that if deaf children are encouraged to sign from an early age, they will most certainly find it to be easier than lipreading and speaking. They will then probably lose their chance of possessing clear speech, or have unintelligible speech, by taking the line of least resistance and signing non-stop. To the school nothing mattered more than clear speech and every attempt was made to ensure pupils had a good command of spoken language by the time they left the school. This required hard work from both the teacher and the pupil. But the result was that the children at Mary Hare were disciplined to speak, even outside the formal classroom, rather than to sign in order to further their chances of being more fully accepted into the hearing world.

My own views on sign language differ somewhat. I feel that although few things matter more than clear speech, deaf people should not be made to reject sign language entirely. Nor should they be made to feel ashamed of it.

Sign language is extremely expressive and one sometimes wonders why man chose to use speech instead. It may be due to the fact that sign language is useless unless attention has been gained, and because signing requires exclusive use of limbs usually adapted for other essential functions.

Wherever possible I feel that deaf people should possess all possible means of communication since it is the ability to communicate which matters far more than anything else. I would prefer to see a deaf person communicate by sign language than not to be able to communicate at all. And I *hate* seeing deaf people being made to feel small by the fact that they only sign.

I am not happy if somebody actually speaks to me using what is known as Total Communication (lipreading, signing, speaking and facial expressions all at once) because I find that if the speaker moves his hands about excessively while I'm trying to lipread him it only serves to make lipreading more difficult. I can either watch the hands *or* lipread – not both. Yet this is probably only due to the fact I have not been brought up to it and I do not dispute its usefulness in the case of people who are unable to lipread very well. On the other hand enforced lipreading may be a good idea at first since it will become easier as more experience is gained. In lipreading, 'practice makes perfect'.

I usually speak normally while talking to hearing people or deaf people who lipread and look down on sign language, or who do not know how to sign. But if I find myself in the company of deaf people who adamantly refuse to lipread the entire conversation I am more than happy to converse in sign language and I refuse to feel that 'signing is always totally bad'. The important thing is to communicate, no matter how. If a German person went to France unable to speak French and found that speaking German was 'just not done' and sneered at, he would be totally cut off. Matters would be even worse if a French person who could speak German refused to speak it to him and insisted they converse in French. To discriminate against sign language users seems to be me totally unfair and only exacerbates the handicap.

Hearing people can learn as many languages as they like. Some speak several. I know of one teacher at Tormead who spoke twelve fluently. So why discriminate against deaf people who only want to master two – a spoken language and sign language? Why should they not have both?

If I am holding a conversation in sign language and hearing

people stop to stare, it doesn't really worry me. Those people would probably stop and stare at anything which is the least bit unusual anyhow.

I am lucky, for my speech is intelligible and my use of sign language an added advantage. The people I feel sorry for are those who can only sign and hence can only communicate with other sign-language users. This limits them to one group alone. Where speech is the language of millions, sign is the language of no more than thousands. Hence the deaf person who only communicates by sign language finds himself in what seems like a deaf ghetto.

If they are content, fine, but if not, I can understand how frustrated some of them may feel at not being able to communicate verbally and normally with hearing people who have no knowledge of sign language. I have never ceased to thank my mother for my ability to speak clearly which means I can do simple things like walk down the road and buy a dress all by myself which somebody who cannot speak will probably find more difficult to do. At the same time, my communication is not limited to speech users alone. I am also able to communicate with those who do not use speech. So I suppose you could say I have the best of both worlds. But it is only recently I have begun to think along those lines. Until round about a few months ago I felt pulled in both directions, unable to make up my mind which was best and unsure as to where I actually belonged.

There is so much fur flying at the moment as to whether children should be taught using sign language or by aural-oral methods. The classic defence of oralism relies on the example of deaf individuals who, despite their handicap, have become outstandingly successful members of society. These 'real successes' are people who, in spite of grave hearing impairment, nevertheless have achieved a level of oral communicative ability which virtually frees them from their hearing handicap; so that they achieve a dual or professional status equal to that of more successful hearing people. The defence of sign language is that it is a mode of communication which involves fingers, arms, facial gestures as well as hands, all of them viable. Hence it is as easy for a deaf child to acquire sign language in a signing home as it is for a hearing child to acquire speech. It emphasises a visual mode of language which, unlike lipreading, provides a linguistic signal which is easily perceived. Furthermore, no special equipment is needed to converse in sign language whereas oral schools spend a great deal of money on acoustic equipment. But I greatly doubt if there can ever usefully be a unified set of principles suitable for educating all deaf children. Enough said.

I started my education at the Mary Hare Grammer School for the Deaf on August 19th 1975. I cried when my mother left me but she cheered me up by giving me a one pound note 'to buy a supply of paper hankies with' . . . and then cried herself all the way home! We were quits. My first night was torture as I was in a dormitory of six, three of whom were in the year above us and all seemed to know what to do while we three were onlookers. I was very homesick but fortunately it only lasted a short while.

For our first lesson we were asked to write a short essay about ourselves and our families at home. This was too much for one girl in the class from Norfolk who, feeling very homesick, burst into tears right away. Our form teacher, who had five children herself, proved to be very human and comforted the girl in such a manner that we all cheered up. All the teachers seemed much more willing to align themselves with us. They did not keep such a formal distance from us as had been the case at my previous schools. This was important because we then felt that they cared about us as we were much more willing to accept their guidance.

It was my first French lesson which really confirmed my opinions about the school, however. At my previous schools I had tried to do French, but had always been forced to give up because the teaching was done by audio-visual methods. That is to say a voice spoke in French from a tape recorder while the class watched a film script and joined in, in chorus, when required to do so. Hence I was excused French lessons and spent the time instead having piano lessons with my form mistress. I enjoyed these as she was one of the kindest, most gentle people I have ever known and she also had a great sense of humour. We laughed a lot. Otherwise, I helped with the junior ballet classes demonstrating the steps they had to execute. I believe I taught Camilla once or twice. For the rest of the time assigned to French, I read books or worked quietly on my own. Although I enjoyed not having to do the great mountains of French homework which the other girls complained about, at the same time I was very envious of them. I was an onlooker and I felt isolated and frustrated at not being able to do something simply because I was deaf.

At the Mary Hare this all changed. I suddenly found I could lipread the teachers and that I could do French. The teachers were always more than ready to write words on the blackboard which we did not understand by lipreading or aural comprehension and this made the great difference as far as French was concerned. We were treated to an amusing episode in our first French lesson, for the little girl who had cried that morning burst into tears again, much to the teacher's alarm. She came over and asked what the matter was, and the girl replied that she simply couldn't do French. The teacher patiently explained that it always seemed very difficult at first. She told us that there was no reason why we could not learn a foreign language just because we were deaf. But the girl couldn't accept this and continued to insist that she could not do French. The teacher asked her to explain this and was somewhat disconcerted when the girl announced 'she could only do German' which she had learnt at her previous school. I've never seen a member of the teaching staff so taken aback.

For many subjects I had to start right at the beginning. One of these was maths and I found myself being told to recite my two times tables at the age of eleven! We then went through all the basic principles again such as decimals, fractions, long multiplication, long division and elementary algebra. This dead ground was re-crossed in such detail that I finally formed the firm foundation which I had lacked before owing to my inability to lipread my former maths teachers, and to an inner dislike of the subject.

I remember the odder things about my first few years there, far better than I do the day-to-day routine events. There were some rather unusual rules, such as the one which forbade anybody to fold their bread in half at mealtimes. One even had to peel oranges in a certain fashion and any other method was considered bad manners. There was a fourpence fine for being late for breakfast, threepence for lunch and twopence if one was late for high tea at 5.30 p.m. On the other hand if you were late for milk and biscuits at 7.30 p.m. somebody else just pinched your share.

Discipline at the table was quite strict and the children were made to eat what they were given, no matter if they disliked it. This led to battles between myself and the matrons when I steadfastly refused to consume soft eggs with runny yokes. I hated them and still do. The soft runniness of the yolk seemed to me unpalatable in the most disgusting way possible. In my first week, I was made to sit in front of a poached egg which I refused to eat for an hour-and-a-half before I was allowed to go without eating it. I did not mind being made to eat other foods which I was not too keen on such as liver, jam tart, and steamed sponge puddings, but I drew the line at soft runny eggs. I must have exasperated the matrons because no other pupil was as consistently stubborn as I was over that one particular food.

In November it was announced that the First Form were to do potato picking. This happened every year. The form above us piled us high with horror stories about the event. They told us how soldiers stood round the fields and watched us with guns in their hands. They expounded gruesome stories of how much your back ached and how you were made to walk five miles back afterwards carrying sackfuls of spuds. We even had it on good authority that you were beaten as you walked along. We were terrified beyond belief and as the day drew nearer we constructed elaborate mental plans which would enable us to escape this dreadful misfortune. The more religious among us prayed, while we nagged them to pray harder, but it was to no avail. One girl in my dormitory broke her leg the day before and was therefore excused much to her relief and she waved us off cheerfully as we boarded the coach bound for our doom. We vowed to make her go next year with the First Form somehow. Our headmaster entered the coach temporarily to tell us all to behave and to work hard at picking potatoes – it was good for us, he said. The harder we worked, the quicker our service to the community would be over. He checked we were all wearing Wellington boots and anoraks for it was 'muddy work indeed'. Meanwhile we were told to arrange ourselves in groups of five.

It was getting dark as we drove off. We wondered how on earth we were supposed to pick potatoes in the dark. Maybe light was bad for root vegetables, we decided. We prayed we would at least be given torches.

The coach pulled into some army barracks and came to a halt. The driver put the brake on and lit up a cigarette. We all assumed this was our cue to disembark and miserably we did so, noticing that there seemed to be a lot of people there besides ourselves. Outside, a group of soldiers was waiting for us, and I realised cautiously that they did not carry guns. Neither did they look 'all horrid and wicked' as we had been informed by some sadistic Second Formers.

Each soldier took a group of five and our group found themselves with a broadly smiling man who said 'Stop me if you can't lipread me'. We awaited instructions as to where the potato field was, but he did not say anything beyond general chat.

In the end a girl in our group plucked up the courage and said, 'Where do we go to pick the potatoes? Where are all the sacks and spades and things?' The soldier threw back his head. 'Potato picking?!' he exploded, and roared with laughter, pulling out sparklers from his pocket as he did so. 'It's a bonfire party, you bunch of half wits.' We were still not wholly convinced. He lit our sparklers, produced toffee apples and led us over to a huge bonfire which had formerly been obscured from sight. We suddenly realised that it was in fact November 5th. In our worried state we had completely forgotten.

'See the Guy Fawkes on the top,' he told us. We looked up and sure enough there was a guy on the bonfire. 'Do you believe me now?' We were so thrilled it was unbelievable. It was one of the best surprises I have ever been subjected to.

The soldier then gave us unlimited supplies of hot dogs, hamburgers and cans of coke plus more sparklers. He next led us over to a shed where we sat down on benches at the front with several other children and were entertained for an hour by Mickey Mouse, Donald Duck, Tom and Jerry and their friends. After this we were taken back outside where our soldier gave us hot jacket potatoes, grinning broadly as he did so. 'Are these the potatoes you picked while I was watching the films?' he asked jokingly. We found this very funny.

After this, came the firework display which was expertly organised and on a very large scale. These were real fireworks – not those puny ones which can be bought in confectionary shops. We screamed when rockets went off and positively yelled as the Catherine Wheel speeded up. All the time there were sparklers and more sparklers for us to play with, and more and more food was given to us to eat.

By the time the evening came to an end it was very late and we were all very tired. We said goodbye to our soldier, who made one last joke about 'potato pickers', and went back to the manor house by bus where the matrons were waiting up to put us to bed, grinning from ear to ear. As we went into our dormitory the girl with the broken leg asked us if it had really been as bad as expected. How delighted Caroline and I were to tell her all about what she had missed. Served her right for laughing at us in the first place! Poor girl – she must have been mad with frustration at missing such a good outing.

Surprises like this were common to the First Form. Another such event was the school's Christmas Party for which the assembly hall was transformed entirely by decorations. The senior school would choose a theme for the Christmas Party and it was all kept a secret from the juniors, especially the First Form. When we all finally burst into the hall that first year we found ourselves in a kind of Disneyland. The standard of the decorations was indeed extremely high and some of the characters actually looked lifelike. There were Snow White and the Seven Dwarfs looking over the balcony at the back of the hall. Donald Duck and Mickey Mouse adorned the walls while the Peter Pan characters occupied the backs of the closed curtains. Tom and Jerry were seen to be engaged in fighting a great battle at the back of the hall. The Christmas tree in the corner was covered with tinsel and fairy lights while paper chains and balloons festooned every square inch of the ceiling.

It was a superb party with an enormous buffet supper. In the middle of everything, Father Christmas (our Principal in disguise) came out of Aladdin's Lamp in a puff of smoke and began distributing presents. He had to take his beard off while he called out our names: we couldn't lipread him with it on. The staff did a little play and so did the prefects. These were very funny as we were so unused to seeing the teachers really let their hair down. Later on, we all sat round while Mr Pearce played the piano in the holly decked Manor Hall: we sang carols while munching Christmas cake. When at last we were put to bed, Mr Pearce came round tucking us all in and gave us each a goodnight kiss! Meanwhile, the party turned into a disco for the older pupils and continued far into the night. I also remember being taken to the Oxford pantomime in January while I was in the First Form. And in the second year we were treated to a day trip to France. In short, we were given an exceedingly good time.

Like all boarding-school children, we revelled in a nocturnal pleasure commonly referred to as 'Midnight Feasts'. These were held in the shoe-cleaning room down in the cellars. We used to stay awake by means of a rota until the dot of midnight, when everybody would be woken up to make the long and dangerous journey down two flights of stone stairs to the cellar. To get to the stairs we had to cross a landing on tiptoe, past two rooms which were occupied by matrons. This was usually where we came unstuck and got caught: we couldn't hear the floorboards creaking.

Other nocturnal amusements were called 'fire practices', in which Mr Pearce would set off the alarm and we would be evacuated from the building as quickly as possible to assemble in the hall for a roll call. At one time I used to think he took a positive pleasure in getting us all up in the middle of the night. These excursions were held at least once a term and we were woken either by the noise of extra-loud bells or by flashing lights which came on automatically when the alarm was activated. At first they seemed very exciting and we loved them but after a while they became a bore. A necessary bore.

All the pupils at the Mary Hare were either approaching adolescence or actually going through the whole process. Adolescence and dating can bring home a handicap such as deafness in a new way. Feelings of isolation and inferiority can act as potentially inhibiting forces when a deaf person forms a relationship with a hearing member of the opposite sex.

The problem is a psychological one at root, but it has concrete effects which may sound silly to hearing people. Sweet nothings whispered in the ears are often infuriatingly meaningless, and it is impossible for a deaf person to join in with hearing contemporaries when they talk about how they 'chatted for hours on the telephone' to a boyfriend or girlfriend the night before. Candlelight dinners can be a nightmare and not at all romantic since the flickering light of the candle is often inadequate for lipreading. Even normal conversation can be a strain: it can rarely be spontaneous. The deaf person has to put down knife and fork – or paper or book or washing-up things or whatever the context requires – simply to concentrate. It may be necessary to move physically in order to see the other person's face clearly. Conversation can't continue at intimate moments unless the lights are on. Constraints like these can place a severe strain on any relationship between a deaf and a hearing person. This in turn increases the feeling of isolation inflicted by the handicap.

No wonder, then, that members of the deaf community often marry each other. They find it more relaxing and reassuring to be with people who understand the problems only too well, and with whom they can communicate easily and share the difficulties. Any 'normal' hearing boyfriends that I have been out with have all had to give just that little bit extra and to make allowances for my deafness. Most of them have adapted without being aware of it, but a few have found it too much to cope with. It may have irritated them to have to repeat things or to have to face me while speaking. It can be difficult having to take trouble over drawing me into their circle of friends instead of me being able to join in spontaneously. Or the friends may find me a nuisance and resent me.

But there are some advantages. Since boyfriends have to make more effort, you can be sure they feel you are worth it. You know they like you enough to take the trouble. Some men find it interesting to have a girlfriend who is different and who has something to say for herself in spite of it. There are times when it is delightfully convenient to be a deaf girlfriend like during a row: I can just close my eyes and say what I have to say, which means that *he* is temporarily unable to answer back. And the 'phone can be put to good use: I had one boyfriend who would never listen to me, but I could always go home and ring him up. Upon sensing the receiver being raised at the other end, I would issue my viewpoint vehemently. He could never argue back, as there was no way I could hear him if he did.

Before I was about fifteen, I rarely used to admit to boys that I was deaf. I thought that if I did they would walk away from me and I was scared of this happening. I once kissed a boy goodnight outside our front gate and we were getting fairly passionate when . . . my hearing aid gave out a loud whistle.

The poor boy jumped about ten feet and asked what the noise was. I didn't want to admit to my hearing aid so I mumbled something about it being the dog. He looked me straight in the face and patiently explained, 'Dogs just don't make noises like that!'

I then told him in an outburst of fury that I was deaf and had to wear a hearing aid. I pointed out that I hadn't wanted to tell him but if he wanted to walk away, he could do so on the spot. I didn't care, I announced categorically. He could laugh at me if he liked. After all, it wasn't my fault that I had to wear the thing. He waited until this storm had subsided and then confessed that he was supposed to wear spectacles for reading but hated them because he felt people would tease him if they knew. I realised how stupid I had been all along.

Now I tend to tell most people that I am deaf fairly early on in an acquaintance. Otherwise, it is a bit unfair on them. I make exceptions of fleeting acquaintances and people I only meet once when I'm unlikely to see them again. Nor do I generally tell people I am deaf straight away: I just introduce the matter naturally into a conversation or use 'Oh, by the way . . .' tactics. I relish moments when they are surprised and refuse to believe it. At least, I like people to have a few minutes to begin to get to know me first: I don't want there to be any danger of their being even the least bit prejudiced right from the start, even if they were eventually to overcome it.

I did have deaf boyfriends at the Mary Hare, and vividly

remember being discovered in an amorous imbroglio in the cellar by a member of the staff who had gone down there to look for cleaning materials: he'd only been wanting to clean his motor-bike!

Such were the callow ecstasies of my career in the junior forms at the Mary Hare. Life in the senior school, from the fourth form upwards, was to be radically different.

CHAPTER ELEVEN

I Lose My Best Friend

For a start, the summer holidays before I entered the Fourth Form were a disaster. Our house at Charterhouse was to have an extension built onto the kitchen which was to be done while we were away in France. The moment we left, they pulled a brick wall down making the house temporarily uninhabitable.

Our stay in France was cut short; it only lasted five days instead of six weeks. My mother was seriously ill and had to be flown back to hospital to England, so it followed that we children came back too. Our house was in no fit state to be lived in and we all had to go and take over the school sanatorium. To begin with it was fun. We slept in hospital beds and there were radios plugged into the wall above our heads which one listened to through plastic earpieces. Our meals were all cooked for us and there were comics to read, TV programmes to watch and the school's sports facilities were easily accessible. We did such things as swimming and squash to fill in time. But gradually the seriousness of the situation had a sobering effect. I was told my mother was definitely about to die and would probably be dead by the end of the week. With a shock I realised it was Thursday. A friend of my mother's tried to explain it to me by telling me that it was going to be easy for my mother to die, but that it would be hard for those people she left behind. It was up to us, she said, to make Mum's last few days happy.

I couldn't believe all this. I had known she had cancer for a long time, but I had thought the chemotherapy treatment she was receiving was working. The idea of life without her was totally inconceivable. We were allowed to visit her once a day and for a while she looked worse each time we saw her. Dad spent most of his time at the hospital while we kept ourselves busy.

Miraculously she did not die, however, and came out of hospital four weeks later making medical history as she did so. I believed the danger to be over and since the worst stage of her illness seemed to be over I was convinced that she would now get better. I didn't dare appear too optimistic, however, in case she 'got ill again'.

Never idle, my mother wrote a nativity play while she was in hospital that summer. It was based upon a group of school children talking about going away for the census where they would all be counted. It had all the usual amusing children's remarks in it. Then it showed Mary and Joseph going to Bethlehem and so forth. Once out of hospital, my mother supervised the children of the Charterhouse masters in rehearsals and for a while she was able to attend the rehearsals herself. Gradually she was forced to stay at home in bed and the wife of my future English master stepped in to help. The date was fixed for the performance which was to be held in the Founders' Chapel at Charterhouse on 9th December. I came home for the weekend from the Mary Hare for the event and the whole family attended save my mother. She was by now almost permanently in bed. The next day, however, she listened to tape recordings of the play, which she savoured, especially when the audience laughed at her jokes, and saw some photographs which had been developed extraordinarily quickly.

She died during that following night.

I hesitate to go into details. Small consolations for a terrible bereavement aren't truly comforting. Yet it all seemed so well timed. She had lived to see the successful production of her play. Robert had just got into Trinity College, Cambridge, and the rest of us were all doing well at school. And although sad, we were relieved that all her suffering was over, and that she had not been in any pain when she died. We were all especially grateful to our family doctor who visited her often and managed to give her enough medication to stop the pain, but without making her at all drowsy. We were also extremely lucky to find such a good friend in the wife of one of the housemasters. She nursed my mother through that last week and was constantly there and available without being obtrusive. This enabled my mother to die in comfort, at home, and not in a lonely hospital bed.

Her death had an immediate effect on me. I no longer had anyone to give me the same guidance, encouragement and support as she had done. Parents are human beings whose lives are physically and mentally linked to their children. Women rear large families and fathers earn the money necessary to support them. It all seems quite bland, quite pat.

A mother, however, plays a transcendent role, hard to define, impossible to analyse. It is she who teaches her child the first lesson in life. My mother was especially lovely as it was she who gave me motivation – especially during those important first few years after I suddenly went deaf – to lead as full a life as possible in the hearing world. A fiery, temperamental person would have been of no use at all. Only patience can help a child through the colossal shock of going deaf. People will never know what she really did. She cheered me up when I was sad, she played with me when I was glad and she was always ready to talk to me and help me widen my spoken vocabulary. She taught me all I know about other people and their problems. There is no friend like a mother.

Edith Whethall, the otologist, whose genius achieved a lot for deaf children, always used to say that when examining a deaf child she wanted first of all to know about the child's mother. Next, she wished to know the child's intelligence and last of all the evidence of the audiogram. This shows how important a mother's influence can be. My mother had great determination. 'Jessica *will* talk,' was her way of thinking – not an unrealistic, 'Oh, she'll be okay – they all said she'll get along fine.' She accepted my handicap, learned all she could about it, equipped herself with a realistic scale of ambitions, and adjusted to having to work hard with me to regain my level of speech. Teaching a deaf child takes a great deal of time and parents must keep their sense of proportion. I, as the deaf child, was important to my mother, but so were the other children. Some parents get so eaten up with ambition for the success of the deaf child that the siblings are neglected and the handicapped child receives far too much attention. At the same time, mother has to run the home, cook, clean, wash and feed. To this day, I honestly don't know how mine did it all.

Besides running a busy home, she somehow managed to keep my specialist appointments regularly and punctually, kept my hearing aids in good working order and worked regularly with me at my speech day in, day out. This is of vital importance. It is no good if the parents only work with the child spasmodically as the mood takes them. It is noticeable that even regular and determined speech therapy sessions are lost on a bright child whose parents are unco-operative. My mother created a pattern of orderly living which provided a firm basis for my learning. Lipreading is understanding a pattern on the face. A child learns these things most speedily when life has a predictable pattern.

This does not mean that the 'predictable pattern' has to become boring. Parents who are lively, outgoing, positive and communicative, and who enjoy time spent with their deaf child, are at a great advantage. My mother had a vibrant imagination and was particularly good at seeing an object or situation from a fresh angle so that she could teach me something new all the while even if the daily routine was not wildly exciting. I can give a very simple example of this.

My mother and I had to go to London frequently to attend clinics and see doctors. This meant commuting from Northwood by tube at fairly regular intervals. My mother seized the opportunity to teach me several things and I could use the underground train system by the time I was ten. She used to show me where we were on the map – say, Sloane Square – and tell me to take her to Blackfriars only a few stops along the Circle Line. This was fairly simple: I only had to read the station signs. Later on she tightened up her standards and made the routes involve changes. The point was that she did not herself give me any help in finding the way. She would say something to me along the lines of:

'Let's imagine I'm a robot. I can't see, hear or speak but you have to look after me and deliver me to Dr Who. He is at Swiss Cottage, hiding from the Daleks. So get me there quckly.'

Then she would clam up and not speak until we reached Swiss Cottage, where I would get a reward – usually a comic, or book or the promise of my favourite supper. Rarely was I given sweets: that would have been a bad idea for obvious reasons. If I got lost or needed directions, the idea was that I would have to ask the underground staff. This taught me even more: how to speak to them, what to say, to tell them I was deaf. It also broadened my lipreading experience and gave me speech practice. I enjoyed these occasions. They were never arduous as my mother was careful not to over-estimate my abilities but to stretch my mind just enough.

Once at Paddington Station, she rehearsed with me what to do if I was lost or if I missed an important train. This was of great value. I put it to use several years later, when I was eighteen, at Crewe Station while on my way to Manchester from Rugby for an interview at the university. I had to change at Crewe and the train from Rugby was late so I missed the connection. This in turn meant that I would be a good half an hour late for my interview. I was frantic with worry. I went into a 'phone booth and tried to dial my father's secretary to ask her to telephone Manchester for me to explain, but there was no reply. I could not dial the university myself because of the problems of going through a switchboard to an extension. I sat down on a bench and tried not to cry. I was near despair when I suddenly remembered my mother's advice and my mind flashed back to a scene at Paddington Station when I was eight-and-a-half years old.

'Let's pretend you've missed your train, Jessica,' my mother was saying. 'What are you going to do? You're on your own. Pretend I'm not here to help you.'

'Dunno,' I replied.

'Come on. That won't get you home,' she said. 'Remember, Daddy will be waiting to meet you at Moor Park. He'll be very worried if you don't arrive. Go and find the guard's room.'

'But I don't know where it is,' I protested.

'Then ask that porter,' she suggested, indicating one nearby.

I asked him and came back. 'He said, it's over there,' I replied, pointing.

'Let's find it,' my mother said, and off we went with me leading her.

'Now let's pretend I'm a friendly porter,' she suggested when we reached the place. 'I don't know anything about you so you'll have to explain from scratch.'

I began the long, memorised recital.

'My name is Jessica. I've missed the 4:30 train to Moor Park.

Please can you telephone home and tell Daddy I'll be late? I'm afraid I'm deaf but please talk normally to me: I can lipread.'

'What's the 'phone number?' my mother asked.

'Northwood 25750,' I replied.

My mother pretended to dial and speak on a pretend 'phone to my father. Then she turned to me and said,

'What do you say now, Jessica?'

'Oh – what time is the next train, please?'

'5:00 p.m. I've told your father I'll put you on that one,' she replied in a make-believe porter's voice.

I then lapsed into silence.

'What else, Jessica?' she said with a severe face.

'Thank you,' I said quickly and the session was over.

Sitting on the bench now at Crewe Station I seemed to see my mother talking to me.

'Come on, Jessica. Sitting there not knowing what to do is not going to get you to Manchester. Go and find the guard's room.'

I looked up and saw a porter standing a few yards away. I asked him where the guard's room was and he was only too pleased to show me. He pointed it out and walked along with me. I laughed as I closed my eyes momentarily and saw my mother grinning. 'See?' she seemed to be saying.

In no time at all, British Rail had contacted my interviewer to say I'd be late and that it was their fault. They then told me what time the next train was and pointed out the platform. As I left the room, I seemed to see a severe expression on my mother's face.

'What else, Jessica?'

'Oh – thanks a lot,' I said meekly, turning round to the railwaymen. As I closed the door I apologised to my mother's image, which was still visually strong in my mind and thanked her for her training.

I built a barricade around my feelings as my mother's death became imminent and it grew obvious that she was failing. I watched in agony as her world began to disintegrate bit by bit. I did not know then how to talk with her and tell her I knew it was almost over. I knew she was dying. But we did not talk about it. We cluttered life with bedside smiles, trivial chatter and pretended business. I never got round to telling her how much I cared. There was a conspiracy of silence which left each of us alone with thoughts and fears unshared. When the end came I erupted in an emotional and physical upheaval. There were so many things I had left unsaid. I hated the world for taking her away from me before I had a chance to say them. Why not someone else? Why her? My ideas and my understanding seemed to fluctuate day by day. I wasn't sure of anyone or anything any more. I trusted no one. I felt she'd let me down by dying and leaving me to cope on my own without her. One evening she'd been there: a sparkling, vital woman, radiating love, warmth, enthusiasm and happiness, and the next morning she was cold and silent, lying alone in that little room at the end of the corridor never to move or speak again.

As I went in to kiss her good-bye after her death, I noticed some cyclamen by the side of her bed, constrasting strongly with some artificial flowers nearby. If anything is symbolic, they were. All the things that live flowers have – freshness, colour, seasonableness, flexibility – were the qualities my mother had when she was alive. And all the things they haven't got which the fake flowers have – artificiality, lifelessness and that hard set look about them – were the main features of the body that lay before me now. I realised then the extent of my loss. I felt bitter and angry at the sheer waste of her life. She was only forty-seven. I was fifteen.

Much of what happened after my mother's death when I went back to school is too personal to discuss. There is a very fine line between exposing some secrets or making fairly candid confessions and revealing too much so that you have nothing left you can call your own. I am happy to share experiences if they will help the hearing public understand 'what it is like being deaf', but there are some things I wish to share only with those close to me. One must also remember that details about my mother's illness and eventual death are not only intimate to me, but to my whole family. I would not want them upset by what they may regard as intrusions on their privacy.

CHAPTER TWELVE

Outward Bound

My life changed a few months after my mother's death, when I went on an Outward Bound course in mid-Wales, near Towyn, for three weeks in August 1979. Although I arrived at the Outward Bound Centre with another deaf girl to whom I could cling for support, we were immediately split up and put into separate groups. The object of this was to make us come out of our shells and speak to the other hearing students on the course instead of just sticking to each other. It was quite true that had I been able to talk to Gail all the time I would have virtually ignored most of the other girls in my group on the specious grounds that I found them difficult to lipread. As it was, I had to persevere and keep trying while at the same time educating them to 'speak properly to me'. It was very good for me, since I had now been at Mary Hare for four years and was a bit too used to people looking at me all the time while also speaking clearly. Suddenly I found myself in a group with nine other girls who had never met a deaf person before and none of them had any idea about how to speak to me. They either mumbled in an embarrassed fashion or spoke far too slowly, exaggerating their mouth movements grossly as they did so. This only made them even more difficult to lipread since it distorted the normal speech patterns and made the atmosphere doubly awkward for both parties.

The first two days were awful. The rest of the group all seemed to get to know each other much more quickly than I did. I was a frustrated onlooker, unable to join in their conversations, unable to make them understand that I wanted to converse *with* them and not to them, unable to obtain any positive feedback in any form, and unable to participate in the 'after-lights-out' chatter in the dormitory. Nobody seemed to know quite what to do with me and I didn't have the nerve to tell them. For the first time, I began to feel angry at my deafness, to such an extent that I started to have worrying visions about my future life. What if I was never able to mix with hearing people? What if I had to be segregated in a deaf ghetto for the rest of my life? I really started to think of myself as a handicapped person instead of a person in my own right who, by the way, happened to have a handicap in the form of deafness.

I did find a friend, however, in one girl in the group. She was called Claire and she had worked with various kinds of disabled people before and could see just how frustrated I was getting. She tried telling the others that I was 'quite normal really', but they still felt embarrassed and didn't quite know how they were supposed to react to my deafness. Hence by the third day I was really reaching a point where I simply couldn't continue in the same fashion for three more weeks. Something drastic was going to have to happen, and it was going to have to happen soon. I couldn't bear the tension any longer.

It is hard for you to express the incredible frustration and desperation I often felt, but if you can imagine being different in a way that sets everybody else apart, it would really leave you feeling very ugly and downcast. Sometimes I would pray to heaven that I could just turn the clock back and start my life all over again. Believe me, that's how you would be feeling. I know, I felt just like that. But I had to stop myself getting too bitter and depressed in the end.

This is how I managed to do it, and in fact it was far easier than I thought it would be. On the evening of the third day I was miserably making the tea for our group in the kitchens and I involuntarily caught sight of my reflection in the mirror. I was fairly disgusted with the girl I saw, so I gave her a long talking to:

'You're a fine one aren't you? Just because you're deaf, you sit there blaming everybody else under the sun for it. As if it mattered! You think that just because you're a little bit weak in the ears your whole life is automatically wasted and that's it. Well, I'm telling you, young lady, *you* should know all about wasting your life – you're really going the right way for that. And it isn't your handicap or your mother's death that's causing it. You're doing this to yourself.'

After that, I decided I was going to take a really long, hard look at myself. A handicap is as big as you allow it to be and I decided that I was not going to let my deafness stop me from having a good three weeks on this course.

It was a very simply executed plan. I just picked up a chair from the kitchen and walked out to where the rest of the group were sitting. I then plunged right into the centre of their social circle, put down the chair and sat on it hard. I told them, 'Now listen, you lot. You can't ignore me just because I'm deaf any longer', and I waited.

They were amazed. Some people looked away or at each other with embarrassed smiles. One girl got up muttering something about a 'phone call. I belted at her at the top of my voice, 'SIT DOWN!' Then I continued.

'I want to talk with you and join in instead of being the passive parasite I feel at present. So I'm going to talk and if you don't answer I shall get GET VERY VERY ANGRY.' One girl told me I was being difficult and that being deaf I shouldn't have come on the Outward Bound course. She was instantly rebuked by Claire who told her *she* was being difficult and also extremely narrow-minded. One by one the rest of the group joined in and told her to give me a chance. She was suitably chastened and mumbled an apology. Furthermore the rest of the group, having stuck up for me, seemed less uncomfortable than before. We now had a common alliance, 'Why don't you ask me questions?' I proposed, 'and if you stop I will start asking you questions but some of them might be very embarrassing.' The last two words were said in a more threatening tone than the rest.

There was no need for me to do anything else after that. They bombarded me with questions and I was not given a break. Later Claire told me that they had been so surprised at just what I had done to make them notice me, they couldn't bear to think what sort of intimate questions I might ask them straight out in front of everyone else, given half a chance.

After this I got on really well with the other girls in the group and they all became much more understanding about my deafness. If an order was issued (or even more important a warning) they made sure that I heard it. The problem was that often neither member of the group would trust another to tell me so I ended up getting the same order relayed to me nine times in a row.

On our fourth day, we were sent into groups of five and each group was taken by van and abandoned at half-hourly intervals some five miles from the centre. We were given maps and told our position. The object of the exercise was that we found our way to a given spot situated six miles away from our present position (and three miles from the centre) where we would be met by the van at a special time. If we were late, they warned us, the van could just leave us to find our own way home on foot. We got worried. The walk was not along tarmac roads. It was all over hills, open areas and rugged footpaths.

There was no getting out of it, so we set off along the route which we had been told to follow. It was the most difficult route that could possibly have existed from A to B. It deliberately avoided all roads and major footpaths. Furthermore, in order to ensure that we stuck to the instructions, we had to 'sign in' at various checkpoints along the way. The latter were tins with screw top lids which enclosed a form which you signed to certify you had reached that point. There was no room for deceit as we sorrowfully found out.

After an hour or so, it started raining really hard and a terrific argument started up in our group when one rather strong-willed police cadet refused to believe that there were no more check points until we reached Carn March Arthur. We won in the end, however, and told her to shut up while we plodded on feeling like clowns in our waterproof clothing. We eventually met up with several other groups. It proved to be a disaster as everyone started arguing about the navigation. We went round and round in circles getting more and more fed up until we realised with horror we had to do a mile in five minutes if we were to catch our bus. Ever heard of the five minute mile done in waterproof clothing? We dropped everything, including our good intentions to stick to the chosen route, and just ran for the nearest road. We reached the top of a hill and – oh joy! oh bliss! – we saw one of the buses waiting on the road at the bottom. We scrambled from the slope at neck breaking speed only to find it was another group and we had to walk.

An outburst of swearing resulted. None of us believed it and thought it was just a trick to frighten us. We thought the bus would be hiding just around the corner with our instructor grinning from ear to ear. However, after turning many corners we resigned ourselves to the fact. What else could we do? I announced my imminent death! Rain poured down and wind cut through us as we 'bravely' struggled on. When at last we came in sight of the centre we nearly wept with relief. But it taught us a very important lesson that applied to life in general. If you make an arrangement to meet somebody, and you are late because of your own incompetence it is unreasonable of you to expect them to wait for you. On a more general level you can say that a 'shoddy performance merits no reward' and that applies to an extremely wide spectrum of affairs. After this, we pulled our socks up.

Although we did a wide range of activities, the course included a lot of walking. We found the Welsh people in general were so friendly that I came to be fond of the place very quickly. Everywhere we went, people whom we had never met before greeted us cheerfully with remarks about the weather, our journey, their journeys and best wishes for a good day. It did not matter where you met them or who they were. We were treated with equal courtesy by all, ranging from a lonely farmer in a field of sheep to an elderly couple sitting on a bench under some trees in the middle of town. These comments really cheered us up and kept us going. Sometimes when it was cold and raining and when we still had five miles to go, it was hard to remain cheerful. At times like these somebody would come up with an idiotic comment every five minutes or so such as 'not far now'. Failing that, people would keep mentioning hot showers, hot food and drink, in an effort to speed up the pace. Needless to say these attempts didn't work and were all booed at in a friendly, or unfriendly, manner depending on the present mood within the company.

Sometimes we would be out on the hills for three or more days walking and camping. After these stretches of utter discomfort it was heavenly to return to the centre once more. I recall that often I was simply only too glad to get rid of that wretched 30 lb rucksack and nurse my bruises, or to crawl into a warm bed and not a damp sleeping bag. I would swear that the next time I got fed up with our electric cooker at hime, I would remember instead that blasted primus stove with a mind of its own. I vowed to be more grateful next time I felt like going to bed that I did not have to put a damp tent up before I could crawl inside. But perhaps the maddest thing was, that in spite of all the discomforts, I loved it. I loved being outside all day amongst beautiful scenery. I loved to see contrasting clouds and different layers of light on hilltops.

Often I was grateful for the fact that I was deaf. Before you raise your eyebrows so high that they reach your hairline let me explain why. Some of the paths were so narrow they forced us to walk in single file. This meant I could not communicate with the others since to do so I needed to walk side by side with them in order to see their faces. I could talk to them but I would get no reply. Hence my enforced silence enabled me to see some of the most beautiful scenery which the others missed because they were too busy chatting away to notice. Being deaf does sometimes have its advantages if only you know where to look for them.

The course reinforced my opinion that a sense of humour is in reality a sense of proportion. Without it we could not have survived. There was once an occasion when we had to do a walk on a very tight time schedule. It was imperative that everything should go according to plan and that we were not at all late. With this in mind we set off towards a place called Angler's Retreat, which we expected to take twenty-nine minutes to reach. In fact it took nearly two-and-a-half hours. The boggy nature of the ground forced us to go slowly. It was all extremely dangerous and so our leader refused to let us rush for safety's sake. At this one girl threw herself into a panic and insisted that we must not be late. The leader replied with a 'better arrive late than arrive dead' type answer for some reason we all fell about laughing at the idea of us all turning up at the centre in hearses complete with flowers. We were laughing so hard that Claire dropped the precious map into the river. It was the only one we had. Without it we were lost. For a while we just all stood looking helpless and stunned while the current rapidly swept it away from us downstream. Then suddenly pandemonium broke out as we realised the potential implication of our loss. We all dropped our rucksacks and charged down the middle of the river after it with water coming up to our thighs. It was a curious spectacle. Ten mad shrieking females running down the middle of a river! After much ado we retrieved the vital piece of paper and returned to our belongings. Eventually we found the checkpoint and I quote from our entry onto the official form: 'Expected time – 29 minutes. Time taken – 2 hours 20 minutes. Reason – we chased our map downstream. Bit of fun, eh! P.S. We're soaked!' It must have shaken the straight-laced officials back at the centre quite a bit.

It was also a river which set the scene for the funniest incident of them all. We were in camp by a river and it was getting on for six in the evening. Mandy and I went up to the river bed, which we judged to be quite deep as we could not see the bottom, and sat talking for some time. The current was fairly swift and we threw blades of grass and leaves into the water, only to watch them being swiftly swept away. By the river, some yards upstream, was a tallish tree with a branch that extended over the river itself. On this branch was a single leaf growing out of the bark itself. Apart from this tree there was not much else save grassy banks.

Mandy suddenly dared me to climb the tree and touch the leaf by sliding myself along the branch. When I protested, she called me a chicken. Spurred into action, I performed the task with a great deal of trepidation and a certain amount of difficulty. She just roared with laughter at me from the bank. After I got down, I informed her in a brisk, formal secretarial type manner that it was her turn to perform. Likewise she protested but I made her do it.

Tragedy struck. She fell off the branch into the river with a loud scream. To my horror I realised I could not see her from the surface and there was no sign of her emerging either. I let out a yell that would have put Tarzan to shame and the others came running. By this time Mandy's head could be seen and it was obvious she was struggling. One girl ran off to get a rope, another to get a rug and the rest of us linked arms to venture into the river to fish her out. Mandy was by now screaming and thrashing around. We got a shock when we suddenly realised she was yelling at us to stop. She was telling us not to come near her but to leave her alone. We were arrested in our tracks by puzzlement. Was this a suicide attempt?

'Wait a minute,' she yelled . . . and stood up! The water barely came above her knees. She had been having us on the whole time, trying desperately to hold her breath under the murky water for as long as possible to make us believe she was drowning. I exploded with rage as she clutched her sides with mirth.

The importance of a deaf person keeping a sense of humour cannot be stressed so strongly. If there is one person I cannot stand it is someone who is deaf feeling sorry for themselves just because they are deaf – I do not like anyone to feel sorry for themselves for no reason and deafness is no reason whatsoever. It is absolutely vital that a deaf person thinks positively all the time and keeps looking on the bright side.

There were one or two nasty moments on the course, though. One of these, I can safely say, occurred because of the fact that I am deaf. In about the second week of the course we had a drama lesson which was held in a big room and everybody waited for the instructor (let's call her Jane to protect her identity) in a small room next door. I was absorbed in a magazine while the others chatted away and I did not notice the room go silent. I assumed that when Jane arrived everyone would get up and move into the larger room rousing me as they did. Suddenly Taj gave me a nudge and I became aware of a deathly hush. Jane was standing in front of me asking me angrily if I would mind paying attention to what she was saying.

'Haven't you even been trying to understand me?' she demanded. 'You are so rude to just read a magazine when I'm talking to you.' As for me, I was horrified. I had had no idea she was even there. She accepted my explanation and apology with some displeasure but the episode really made me think. Deaf people must sometimes appear jolly rude to the hearing public. The latter may feel deaf people are ignoring them on purpose and not realise that in fact the deaf person simply has not heard. Another episode such as this occurred during my second year at Charterhouse. A group of first year girls who had only been at the school one week were discussing different female members of the second year and pointing out which of them had been helpful and which had not. One girl happened to mention my name and to say I'd not only told her where the library was but that I'd actually taken her there myself. Another girl asked what I looked like and when given the appropriate description she was heard to say 'Oh my God! I hate that female. She's so rude. I called her from behind to ask her something and she didn't even *bother* to turn round and answer.' When it was pointed out that I was deaf she was aghast. I heard about the story a week later and it really made me wonder how many other people I must have upset at times by behaving like this. The irritating thing is that it is not my fault. Even more irritating is the fact that it can't be helped and so one is always going to be unconsciously upsetting and annoying people wherever one goes.

This raises the presumption that a deaf person will always have practical problems. What if he is crossing a road and does not hear a car coming up behind him out of control? What if he does not hear fire alarms or similar warning sirens? There was always a danger when I was rock climbing on Outward Bound that I would not be able to hear warning shouts if a dislodged rock was in danger of falling on me. In spite of this, however, I enjoyed myself tremendously and emerged alive.

Some people did not benefit from Outward Bound. Some presented characters which were weak, and they cracked under the mental and physical strain despite support from the rest of the group. One such girl in our group invented breathing problems and so she ended up not coming with us on many of our expeditions. In other words, she bowed out. She curried sympathy and pretended to have violent nightmares which left her seemingly unconscious. At first we were taken in by them and we all felt sorry for her until the staff at the Centre told us to leave her alone and to take no notice of her. I think underneath that she was in fact very lonely and wanted attention because she kept coming out with all these fantasy stories. To name but a few, she had twenty 'O'-Levels, was a secretary earning nineteen thousand a year. As the week progressed she revealed 'in confidence' to everyone that she was having an affair with her boss and owned a castle in Bavaria. It was too incredible to believe and the rest of the group quickly lost patience with her which in turn upset her even more. I quote from the diary I kept during the course.

> 'August 29. X had another nightmare. It was awful. Kathy was in tears. Frances took her temper out on X's bed. Claire was fed up and we were all tired. It is the ninth night in a row she has woken us up in the small hours, just for the sake of some attention which she could obtain more easily by behaving normally. The staff have carried her off to the sick room and have told her she is putting a strain on us all unfairly. It's ridiculous. She knows she is pretending and she knows that we know that too. But why is she doing it? I hate sloppy sympathy but I do wish I could help her to help herself.'

I was not angry with her. It was obvious she had some form of a handicap which was difficult to define.

I certainly loved the Outward Bound Course. We did so many different things in just three weeks. We climbed, canoed, camped, performed rope exercises, obstacle courses, orienteering, initiative tests, mock interviews and estate work. We went down mines, we pot-holed, we swam in the sea, we ran cross-country and we walked. As well as all this we produced a full length play for a public audience. I quote further from my diary at the end of the course.

> A few weeks ago I would never have thought I could climb Cader Idris, go down a mine, abseil, rock climb or canoe. I never thought I would ever have the nerve to say Grace in French in front of a whole dining room full of sixty-five hearing people. Neither did I believe I could walk thirteen miles every day for four days in a row with a 30 lb rucksack on my back and not give in. I suppose this is what Outward Bound does to you. It brings you out and encourages you to find your own personality and be what you want to be. Well, I want to be with hearing people again. I want more contact with them than I have at present. Not that I shun the deaf

> world. Far from it, but I do not want my communication to be narrowed down to their secluded world alone just as a gregarious Chinaman would resent not being able to speak to any member of another nationality. Hearing people are not as bad as I used to think they were. They do not want to laugh at me all the time. They want to laugh with me and be my friends.

Needless to say the departure was tearful. We had all got to know each other so well and we had all been through so much together that it was difficult to break up and say goodbye.

CHAPTER THIRTEEN

Times of Trial

I went straight from the Outward Bound course back to school. Term had already started and had been going for around a week before my return.

Of course, I was pleased to see all my old friends and to feel the friendly atmosphere again, but this time something seemed somehow lacking. My experiences on the Outward Bound course, with 'normal', hearing people, had whetted my appetite for the hearing world. I no longer wanted to be segregated at Mary Hare. I no longer wanted to 'have it easy', to be dependent on teachers who spoke extra-carefully for me and to have all my notes printed out for me. I wanted to 'fly the nest'. I wanted to strip myself of my cotton-wool cocoon. I wanted to be independent.

I decided I would *will* myself back into the hearing world. I longed to be among hearing people again: otherwise, my contacts with the hearing would continue to be limited to friends at home or, worse still from my point of view, to boys and girls who visited Mary Hare to play sports matches. A place of my own, an unprotected place, among the big, the bad and the brutal, 'out there' became my goal. The first step was to go to a normal school soon after 'O'-levels to do 'A'-levels in a hearing environment.

I was sure I would cope. The exhilaration of breaking through to my companions on the Outward Bound course, and of forming such strong friendships with some of them, had changed my stereotype of what hearing people were like. They were not all the selfish ogres I had made them out to be in my own mind. For the most part, they were humane and willing to help if only you told them how. The rest now seemed more of a challenge than a threat. There was no need to be shy or frightened of them any longer, and there was no reason to think of them as a breed of supermen, endowed with baffling powers. I had at last experienced for myself, and proved to myself, that the only difference was that their ears worked better than mine.

My plan to go to a hearing school for the Sixth Form was based on the assumption that I was going to have to leave the Mary Hare at some stage anyway. If I left at the end of the Sixth Form to fend for myself, the hearing world might prove too much of a rude shock. On the other hand, if I had two years at a normal school where I'd still have some shelter from the secular blast – at least I'd be housed and fed and wouldn't have to earn a living – I could get accustomed to the outside world more gradually. That, at least, was how I formulated my desire to leave Mary Hare. Inwardly, the desire to do so had become a supra-rational obsession.

Surely, I argued, the aim of the school was to give the deaf pupils a training which would allow them to take their place in the hearing world when they left. I felt the Mary Hare had already done all they could for me and that if I stayed there much longer I would get bored and frustrated. My diffidence about hearing people might return. I announced decisively that I needed a change and that it would be a good idea to make the break now, while I was in a positive frame of mind.

It costs about £10,000 a year to keep a child in a special school. This is due to the high teacher:pupil ratio which is required (1:6 at Mary Hare) and to the expensive audiological equipment. Then there are meals and other residential expenses which most children don't incur. Only a relatively small amount would have to be spent to fit a deaf pupil into the Sixth Form of an ordinary school. To judge from my own experience, only minimal adaptations are required, and it gives young deaf people a helping hand into adulthood. The principle could be extended to other handicapped students, such as those who are blind or in wheelchairs. The economics behind it, the logistics, the social aspects, *everything* points to the integration of handicapped children into ordinary schools, at least in the Sixth Form. And that includes the deaf.

I think the benefits are not confined to the deaf child. Hearing children get something out of it as well. One of the most important things I've found is that failures of communication between the deaf and hearing worlds – and this amounts to total breakdown between many individuals – are the result of long separation. Ordinary children rarely see or meet deaf children: that is why they don't know how to deal with them or react to them.

When they do meet someone 'different', it comes as a shock. They are afraid of the differentness – not so much of the physical thing, but of the possibly different mentality behind it. Even the relatively small differences in behaviour and appearance which distinguish the deaf can alarm an unaccustomed hearing child at first. Deviations from the expected pattern alienate the child. A potential play-mate or schoolfriend who is deaf has to be *expected* in order to be *accepted*.

I wanted to be part of the hearing world no matter how much effort it required. In fact a lot of the necessary effort which I put into my attempts at self-integration is unconscious. Going to sit next to someone to try and talk to them requires a much bigger than average effort on my part but I still have to do it. I have to stop myself thinking, 'Oh God, I've got to be brave because I've got to go and talk to someone.'

If you're deaf, it's just got to be part of you.

Some deaf people, because they've been told they're helpless, genuinely believe they are. They're inhibited from going to talk to someone to the point where they're unwilling even to try. This sort of inhibition is symptomatic of the general disadvantages which deaf people labour under, not just in the context of casual conversation, but in all fields which demand contact with the hearing world – business, employment, shopping, management and administration, even on a domestic scale, and human relationships.

It's not the fault of the deaf, but of those who segregate them in deaf clubs, deaf centres, deaf everything, without thinking about integrating them with 'normal' people. Segregation starts in non-oral deaf schools, and it's in deaf education that the bad consequences of segregation have to start to be remedied.

I'm not saying that there's no place for specialised schools or centres of the deaf. But, if you're deaf, the present emphasis makes you a disabled person in all senses of the word: physically disabled, psychologically disabled, socially disabled. You won't be able to cope without assistance. You must only mix with other disabled people. You're inadequate. You may not be *told* you're inadequate in so many words, but that's fundamentally what you come to believe. Everybody is always telling you how sad it is: it becomes a self-fulfilling prophecy, for it leads to self-pity and so to self-contempt. And there isn't much that's sadder than that.

I'd like hearing people to forgo all pity for the deaf. There's no call for it and no excuse for it. It's totally destructive and negative. It's bad for whoever's doing it and it's bad for the person they're doing it to.

I was already convinced of all this before I left the Mary Hare. I was beginning to be aware that many children with very mild handicaps, like asthma and some forms of epilepsy, are needlessly kept in special schools. I suspected that integration would be the best way to help them. I knew it was the best way to help myself.

I decided that my best course on leaving the Mary Hare would be to try to get a place to do 'A'-levels at Charterhouse, where they have girls in the Sixth Form. The fact that my father was the Headmaster seemed to imply more advantages than disadvantages – advantages of convenience and communication. I wasn't worried about being labelled 'The Headmaster's Daughter'. Several other masters' daughters were at the school. Mine wouldn't be a unique predicament. Furthermore, children of members of the teaching staff were entitled to places, for which competition was stiff, ahead of other candidates, as long as they did reasonably well in the entrance exam.

I admit that I was influenced by the knowledge that my father's support would help me get a place. If anyone thinks I was unfairly exploiting my father's position, I am not going to argue. But I'd have had enormous difficulty overcoming prejudiced opposition at other schools: I knew many teachers would baulk at the thought of a deaf student in their classroom; I was aware that I would encounter opposition on the grounds that my earlier progress at hearing schools had been less satisfactory than at the Mary Hare. If I needed my father's influence to get a place at

Charterhouse, I was prepared to use it and I didn't care what people thought. In the event, it didn't turn out to be necessary.

Once I had made up my mind about changing schools, the first thing I had to do was inform Mr Pearce. I picked my moment carefully. After assembly each morning, which was held in the Dulverton Hall, everybody would file out on the way back to the classrooms. If anybody wanted to ask Mr Pearce anything, it was customary to approach him then, informally. Some mornings there would be nobody who wanted to question him, but more often than not there was a horde of people clustered round him, trapping him and clamouring for attention.

On that particular Thursday morning, I waited until everybody had finished their requests and gone away before I casually sauntered up to him and informed him I wished to hand in my notice! He took it very well.

Unfortunately, my father had misgivings at first. He thought I would be better off at the Mary Hare as my previous experience of hearing schools had not been encouraging. But Mr Pearce generously supported my case for re-entry into the hearing world and, before long, my name was down for an interview at Charterhouse the following November.

I was interviewed by a panel of three people. Two of them were members of the teaching staff. The third was the wife of one of the masters.

I remember being incredibly nervous. What if I couldn't lipread them? What if I was so used to trained teachers of the deaf that I found 'normal' teachers impossible? What if they somehow found an excuse to reject me on account of my deafness? The anxiety made me so tense that I could lipread neither the more elderly teacher nor the woman when they asked me why I thought Charterhouse was for me. I started to panic after two repetitions got me nowhere, until the younger of the two male teachers took over. I sank back in my chair with relief when I found I could lipread him perfectly.

I still wasn't free from anxiety. What if they asked something else that I couldn't lipread? For fear of this, I began to do most of the talking. I talked about all the subjects I could think of, even if they were only marginally relevant. My fear of being unable to understand further questions seemed to galvanise my brain. I 'screwed my courage to the sticking-point' and started to ask *them* questions which I could be more or less sure of making out the answer to. I asked things like, 'How many in a class?' I knew I would only have to lipread a number. Then I tried, 'Will the teachers mind if I always sit at the front?' I knew any polite answer would be in a positive context. Occasionally, the teacher whom I could lipread managed to get a word in edgeways and ask me something. But these occasions were pretty rare and whenever they happened I had little trouble lipreading what was said and answering appropriately.

I did not know then whether the teacher knew what I was doing and why, but I found out two years afterwards. I lived with his family during my second year at Charterhouse and in November he took his daughter for a similar interview for admission to the school. I was chatting with his wife in the kitchen at the time and as father and daughter went out of the back door together, he was heard to remark,

'Remember, Sarah, if *you* talk a lot, they can't ask *you* any questions!' I still grin when I think of it.

My letter of acceptance was given to me while I was working in my room at the Mary Hare. After I read the first sentence, I went mad, yelled, screamed and threw the letter into the air, nearly causing respiratory and cardiac failure in my friends standing close by. I had done it! I had found the means of integrating myself with hearing people once more.

My 'O'-levels were now enlivened by a new goal and I worked harder than I had ever done before. My friends were also pleased for me and egged me on.

My experience of 'O'-levels was pretty commonplace, I suppose, but, like most people, I found it sheer hell at the time. As soon as I came out of one paper, I had to sit down and revise for the next. I'm sure many of those unfortunate enough to have shared this experience will agree that the monotony is the worst part of it. It seems an unending round: revise; get nervous; sit down in exam room; write; rush to finish; revise; get nervous and so on, round and round the vicious circle.

My last few months at Mary Hare passed quickly. We had

an enormous midnight feast a few nights before the end of the summer term and I sadistically told Mr Pearce about it the following day, while he was giving us a ride in his Bentley: This is just one example of how relaxed relations were between staff and pupils at the Mary Hare – the whole atmosphere of the place was friendly and I admit we were sometimes over indulged. But it's nice if it's just *sometimes.*

Otherwise, term ended in the usual way and I went home for the holidays before starting at Charterhouse in September. A workless summer stretched, long and glorious, before me. Life seemed to be looking up. I felt as if nothing could go wrong. But it did.

I was the victim of a hit-and-run driver on 9th August 1980. It was a sunny Saturday afternoon and I was shopping in Godalming. I turned off the High Street by the Post Office and went down Mill Lane towards the railway station, walking on the pavement all the time. Out of the blue, a white van came down the hill, mounted the pavement, and – almost before I saw it – it crashed into me, knocking me backwards against the wall. The wing mirror cracked my head just above my left ear.

Whoever the driver was, he got off scot free, but I hope his conscience is as guilty as hell. The Police didn't catch him. Nobody did. Nobody even managed to get the number of the vehicle. But the damage he did is unforgiveable as far as I am concerned.

The immediate effect was hospitalisation with concussion and shock. But that was just the beginning.

I had confusing police interviews, punctuating the endless streams of pain-killing injections. As the days passed and I became more aware of my surroundings, I noticed that from where I was lying in the hospital bed, I could hear what I took to be a machine making a buzzing noise outside my room. It droned on day and night. There were times when it was louder than others, but it never stopped. I could not work out what it was. It did not seem rational to have such a noisy machine in a hospital, where there were sick people trying to rest and get better. None of the other patients seemed to be bothered by it so I assumed that, sooner or later, I would get used to it.

One day, driven to the point of despair by the unendurable noise, I asked the doctor what sort of machine it was and what it was for. Did it have to be so noisy, I complained. Surely modern technology could have come up with a quieter machine which would do as well. I got exasperated with the doctor. I *ordered* him to switch the damn thing off. It was driving me *mad*.

Imagine my shock and horror when he told me there was no such machine making no such noise. It was all inside my head.

The hit-and-run incident had caused it. It would be the only sound I would ever hear again. And I would probably never be rid of it.

It was, the doctor explained, a condition known as tinnitus. It was connected with a malfunction of the cochlea – that tiny organ in the middle ear, which was transmitting impulses along the auditory nerve to my brain.

Let me explain more clearly. Normally when there is an external noise – that is, originating outside the body – our ears pick up the sound waves and direct them to the cochlea. The cochlea then sends messages to the brain to tell it that there is an external noise. In the case of people with 'good' hearing, the brain may then tell the person what the noise is and where it is coming from. In the case of tinnitus, the cochlea lies like a Cretan. It behaves as if receiving external stimuli and keeps communicating noise to the brain when in fact there is no external noise at all.

That was the type of tinnitus I was suffering from – and still suffer to this day. There are other sorts: tinnitus can include noises in the head caused by blood flowing through constricted vessels to the ears. However caused, tinnitus is an always upsetting, sometimes maddening disease.

There is nothing psychosomatic or hypochondriac about it: let me be quite clear about that. It is an acute physical reality, just as much as a heart attack or a flesh wound. There are actual, physical organs and mechanisms which cause it. It is not 'all in the mind' even though it occurs in the head.

My misery was complete when the doctor told me it was incurable.

I tried to comfort myself with the fact that tinnitus does not develop into something more general, like a cancer or a heart condition. It does not harm the body's health to any great extent. But it is mentally damaging. I believe hearing people can suffer terrible irritation from particular noises: a dripping tap, a passing juggernaut, a repetitious whistle. Imagine that there is no way of ever stopping a noise like that or of getting away from it. Then you will have some idea of what tinnitus is like.

The severity of tinnitus varies. In some people it comes and goes. In others, like me, it is continuous but fluctuates in volume. Some people can wear hearing aids which produce noises and thus help to 'mask' the tinnitus. For me and others like me there is just no stopping it, short of beating yourself unconscious by bashing your head against a brick wall. There isn't really any 'getting used to it' either. It just doesn't settle down for long enough at one consistent level.

When I first got it, I told myself the tinnitus would go away one day. I was wrong. It hasn't. It has persisted and will go on indefinitely. But everybody has to live with something. It may be a guilt complex, insomnia, a 'hang-up' of some sort, a medical condition like diabetes, heart disease, epilepsy. It may be the colour of their skin, their race, their creed, acne or ugliness or a proverbial mother-in-law. It can be anything. It may even be something no one else is aware of. Everybody has his own handicap.

I think it helps to recognise this. The best way to think of a handicap is as a hurdle. If you overcome that hurdle, you feel better and stronger for it. The way you overcome it – and the extent to which you overcome – is a matter of personality. I found it was best for me if I faced my problems and leaped my hurdles, no matter how feeble I felt.

But worse was to come. Until my accident, I had retained enough vestiges of hearing to get some help from the use of an aid. I was looking forward to being able to wear it again. After the periods of concussion were over and the pain had subsided, I turned to my hearing aid with an old friend's welcome. It was only a marginal comfort but I relished even that.

When I put it on, it didn't work. I assumed the battery was flat. I went through a whole packet of new batteries before I realised: it wasn't the aid which was at fault. It was me. I could hear nothing but the noises in my head. I had gone from profound to total deafness.

I went for tests and they told me I was now without any hearing which could be amplified by the use of an aid. The doctors' confirmation of my fears left me devastated. If I had met the driver who knocked me down at that moment I could have killed him.

I told myself not to be silly. There was more to life than just a working pair of ears. I had retained so little hearing for most of my life that total obliteration hardly made much difference. I was lucky. I could already lipread. I knew all about the handicap. I scolded myself out of self-pity by lecturing to my reflection in the mirror. It might have been far worse for a hearing person to be suddenly plunged into an abyss of silence without the long preparation I'd had. God had spared me most of the worst things that can happen to someone who is run over. I could have been killed or – worse, I think – severely brain-damaged. I could have lost a limb or limbs or been seriously disfigured. Far more serious things happen to other people in similar circumstances all the time.

I wasn't totally angelic. At times I rebelled inwardly and had a good mope. But in general I kicked myself out of it. I knew from experience that self-pity only makes things worse.

CHAPTER FOURTEEN

Deaf Girl at Charterhouse

I jumped straight with both feet into my first term at Charterhouse, and right from the start I loved it. It gave me a sort of 'high', a psychological lift. I was living with normal, hearing people again, sharing their activities and being treated like them. I was in a more natural environment with respect to the outside world and I was no longer restricted to the deaf world alone. People spoke normally. There was no sign language or mention of hearing aids to remind me of the fact I was deaf. Not that I wanted to forget it, but neither did I want to constantly remember.

The first thing that struck me about Charterhouse, compared with the Mary Hare, was the greater degree of impersonality that existed. A class consisted of many more pupils than I had formerly been accustomed to. Where was the friendly intimacy of the Mary Hare? The classrooms here were larger and had many more desks arranged for the most part in rows. There was nothing like the former fashion I had known where the pupils were snugly centred around the teacher. Further still, the teachers (or 'beaks' as they were called here) kept themselves more distant than at the Mary Hare. One must remember that they had far more pupils to teach, so it was more difficult for both parties to get to know each other. But it was not only this, the staff did not align themselves with pupils as much as the teachers of the deaf had done. They did not chat generally to us about how a light-bulb had blown in the kitchen the night before, or about how they had burnt the Sunday roast. In other words, they kept more to themselves and did not mix their private life with their job so readily.

I did not mind this, but it often meant I was only able to lipread the staff in classroom situations where they used their 'teaching' voices. If I ever met them outside the classroom and they spoke to me in their 'normal' voices I sometimes found it extremely difficult to follow. Once out of the formal classroom the staff tended to relax. They ceased to speak so clearly and were apt to mumble. They also moved their hands around too much. They would also speak more colloquially which meant I then had to lipread words I'd never seen them say before. If a deaf person can lipread a teacher outside the classroom then it is not too difficult to lipread that same teacher in the classroom. In fact the classroom situation is probably the easier. This is due to the fact that teaching practice requires teachers to emphasise their usual speech patterns, which you already know from informal discussions, whilst explaining facts. When it is the other way round however, it simply does not work. Hence I used to dread meeting a member of Brooke Hall in the cloisters outside teaching hours in case of embarrassment caused by my inability to lipread.

There were ways of solving the problem such as arriving at a lesson a few minutes early on the pretext of asking about some work. This meant lipreading was not too difficult as the situation was in between the two extremes. By this I mean the beak usually adopted a slight teaching voice, because he was explaining something, but retained a lot of the normal speech patterns because it was not essentially a formal classroom situation. Let me point out, however, that very often I did need things explained again which I had missed in class, so this was seen as an effective way of killing two birds with one stone.

I still had problems in this area, and I recall once that after fainting one morning, when I had not eaten properly, I was placed in Great Comp (the school sanatorium), for the day. After lunch my English beak dropped in to see me to ask how I was and I found myself hardly able to lipread him at all. Yet he had taught me for two years. I had rarely met him outside the classroom and I could not understand his normal mouth movements very well, as these were much faster and less clearly enunciated than in class. He found this very amusing and laughed every time I said 'pardon' before giving me up as a hopeless case.

Another thing I noticed about Charterhouse was that lessons got off to a much quicker start. At the Mary Hare we had had to spend the first few minutes of a lesson messing about putting on headphones and other such acoustic equipment, checking it was working, and only then could we begin. Quite often a broken or whistling set of headphones caused further delays. At Charterhouse it was not so. We went in, sat down, opened our books and began work straight away. There was rarely any wastage of time except when boys would introduce red herrings to the beak.

Discipline was different too. At the Mary Hare we had a lot more discipline outside the formal classroom. Our spare time was supervised to a larger extent, we were made to make our beds and eat all we were given on our plate. We had to perform more cleaning duties and other 'fatigues' such as washing up than at Charterhouse. Our bedtimes were earlier and the matron's word was law. At Charterhouse the system within houses was more relaxed. Although one had to ask permission to go to town, there were far fewer formalities connected with the whole business. It was far easier to get away without making one's bed or eating school food. More time was available, too, to watch television and even the most junior boys were able to make tea, coffee and toast whenever they liked. At the Mary Hare this had been a prefect's privilege.

In the classroom, however, the reverse was the case. Classroom discipline at Charterhouse was, on the whole, stricter, with a few exceptions where beaks could not keep control. At the Mary Hare, the formal classroom was by far a more relaxed affair. The atmosphere had been more easy-going and although a lot of work was done, the pace was not quite so hectic or intense. Jokes between the staff and pupils were the norm and were allowed as long as they did not interfere too much with work. 'Illegal' conversations between pupils during lessons were also more common than I found them to be at Charterhouse where one would be quickly silenced. Mind you, we did do a lot of talking at the Mary Hare in silent mouthed language while the teacher's back was turned. A most unfair advantage over our hearing contemporaries, perhaps?

An important question I feel I must ask myself here is how the beaks coped. On the whole I think very well. Some of them seemed anxious at first but it soon wore off. The fact to be aware of, however, was that at a school such as Charterhouse, the pressure on the teaching staff is such that in class virtually no exceptions can be made. It was perfectly reasonable for me to make simple requests such as 'Please face my way when you speak and not at the blackboard' or 'Please do not walk round the hashroom (Charterhouse slang for classroom) so much.' These are good teaching practises anyhow and usually serve to benefit the rest of the class as well. One boy told me that he was now able to understand one of the beaks while before he had had difficulty. I could not, however, expect them to go out of their way to a great extent and revolutionise their teaching just for me.

Yet teachers are human and many of them often forgot. I then felt embarrassed about pulling them up but it was one of those things I had to do. I was grateful for them for always taking it so well whenever I pointed this out to them. One beak in particular was always forgetting and it was usually only the look of intense concentration on my face which reminded him. Sometimes the beak would wander off down to the back of the hashroom and then, feeling uncomfortable under my steady gaze which followed him (once I even physically manoeuvred my chair as a subtle hint) he would realise what he was doing, whereupon he would immediately rush back up to the front with apologies for forgetting. Some deaf people would find this upsetting but I found it highly amusing. In a way it was a compliment to me that they forgot my deafness. It meant they thought of me as a normal pupil. But to say this in no way means I am ashamed to be deaf and was therefore pleased when they forgot it. What I mean is that the fact I was deaf did not prevent their thinking of me as a person in my own right and this gave me a lot of pleasure.

Some beaks did not go out of their way to help at all and continued walking around, mumbling and being generally unco-operative. Fortunately I only had one of these and the rest were extremely helpful. I had one history teacher who began by writing out a brief synopsis of each lesson for me and also by referring chapters of books to me to read. This was a great help and was intended to last until I got used to copying other people's notes. I found a friend in the same 'hash' (lesson or class) who let me copy her notes over her shoulder as she wrote them down. This was one of the most helpful things I have ever had done for me. To relieve the monotony of my just plain copying historical facts, Sophie used to write down quotes from the rest of the hash which had caused laughter. She ensured I never missed any of the fun. I duly copied down these quotes onto my notes and two years later while I was revising for my 'A'-levels, I found them a great help. I kept reading and reviewing my notes in the hope of finding more. Apart from this, I find them funny in their own right. To quote but a few:

Beak: 'What do any of you wishy-washy lot know about the Black Death?'

Boy: 'Idi Amin.'

Another went –

Boy: 'My great-grandfather was in the Burmese War, sir, and he lost a leg.'
Beak (drily): 'Pity it didn't affect him in other ways Jerry.'

Once the beak said that he was 'a man of steel like Bismarck'. A boy then told him, 'I think you are a wishy-washy liberal, sir.' To which the beak retorted, 'There's something about being called wishy-washy which makes us flaunt our aggression even further.' My notes are full of quotes such as these and Sophie and I often spent a lot of our time in such fits of giggles that we did not dare look at each other for fear of cracking.

My English beaks made efforts to slow down and they always told me to stop them if I were unable to follow. Sometimes I did find it difficult but I all in all managed to keep my head above water with Nicola's help. She sat beside me in English and took a great deal of trouble. She pointed to the place on the page, told me page numbers, told me of any work set and if I wanted to know something we corresponded on scraps of paper. She never made me feel inadequate or a burden at all. Yet it was hard for me in many respects for often I only had the written notes and hence missed a lot of verbal background information. This did not deter me to a great extent. I just got a reading list from the beaks and got on with it. I often felt guilty at the way the person next to me had the moral obligation to help me. For this reason, I had to be careful only to ask help from those who I knew could cope with it. It always had to be the same person so that I could get used to their style and also so that I could establish an easy mode of communication. Neither of these things would have been possible if I had had to switch about continually. Some people seemed over-willing to help at first and this was an immediate danger signal. Those characters were usually the ones to tire of helping the quickest. The people who seemed easy-going and who made no fuss when you asked for help were the best since they were often the least bothered at having to adapt their ways. The less hassle made, the better. I was lucky that Mike, Andrew, Anna, Sophie and Nicola were always consistent. If one has a handicap such as I have, one must never be ashamed to ask for help. From my experience it is silly to be too proud and, furthermore, people are always willing to help provided they are asked politely and told exactly what the problem is.

It can't have been easy for the beaks, either. Many of them may have worried that I was merely being polite rather than truthful when I said I could follow the lesson perfectly well, thank you. For some of them it must have been a strain to have consciously to make the effort of speaking more clearly and not walking about so much. Old habits do indeed die hard. One English teacher taught a hash consisting of my contemporaries immediately after teaching mine. Teaching me would often wear him out since he had to make himself stand still in front of me for forty whole minutes. As a result he would then have to teach this next class sitting down with exhaustion.

I made some teachers suffer. One of them had a cold classroom which he heated by the sole means of an electric fan heater. I used to ask him to switch it off as I could feel the noise it made through vibrations it produced which irritated me immensely and disturbed my lipreading concentration. I must admit he was very good-natured about the fact I forced him to freeze.

But I don't feel it is a bad idea for beaks and pupils alike to have suddenly to cope with a handicapped person. In fact the experience probably does them good. Several of my contemporaries said I had opened their eyes to facts which they had before taken for granted. Those who crossed my path while I was at

Charterhouse now know something about the difficulties deaf people have. They will know how to react to a deaf person should they meet one in future instead of curling up in embarrassment. For the beaks, the experience could prove useful.

Zoology practicals presented a problem as often the beaks would deliver points at various times from all over the room. Often, I did not get these unless Charlie or Andrew remembered to tell me.

Some beaks gave me lessons outside the timetable. In other words they reserved one period a week when I could ask them questions about work missed or not understood. I had one in History and one in Zoology. I could have had more if I had asked for and needed them, but these were more than sufficient and the system worked very well. In my second year I lived with the family of my Zoology beak which obviously made him more easily accessible for discussion. We would delve into affairs such as haemoglobin transport or the Bohr Effect at the breakfast table, much to the frustration of the rest of the family.

In fact what it all boils down to is that a deaf person becomes very much dependent on the goodwill of other people. I was lucky. Others have not been so fortunate. Friends, *real* friends, became very important. They are the ones who proved to be the deciding factor in the end. I could not have done it alone and far from trying to hide the fact, I am the first to admit it.

But it must all be give and take. It is no good expecting others to do all the work for you. You must meet them half-way. It is no good a beak giving me extra help unless I am prepared to make use of it. Similarly, it would be no good for them to give me book references if I was not prepared to look them up and read them.

There were difficult times. Often I felt tired and fed up with life in general. Any notes I took during hash were in rough which meant I had to spend somewhere between two and three hours each evening trying to copy them up neatly. Nor was this a simple task. During the actual lessons my eyes were needed for lipreading and therefore seldom if ever left the teacher's face. Hence I could not afford to look down at what I was writing in case I missed some vital point. I wrote blindly – that is to say I scribbled frantically without looking down. The results often looked like Chinese and had to be deciphered before they made any sense to me. All this had to be done before I could even begin to sort out any set work.

But the system had advantages in spite of the hard work involved. The fact that I had to copy my notes out twice meant that I understood them better. They became clearer mentally and I was able to organise my layouts better. I could leave out irrelevant bits, expand and exemplify important areas and, in doing so, I found all the pieces of the jigsaw would slot into place. There was also a valid point when it came to exams. I would know it all better and I would therefore have far less revision to do. But anything worth having often means one has to work hard for it and the self-discipline was certainly very good for me.

I did suffer a bit of abuse, but not much. A fat boy once told me I should be kept at a special school because that was where deaf people belonged. I could never be part of the hearing world he said and someone as deaf as I was should not try to integrate myself with them. He said that deaf people should be segregated because they were a burden on society. I immediately retorted that somebody who was as overweight as he was should be on the sports field trying to do something positive about it because it was a burden on his heart. I'm not saying I won the argument. Both of us were hurt by our remarks. But I did have the last word and I showed him that I was able to hit back. If this kind of thing happens, I feel you can do more good if you stick up for yourself. Either that, or walk away quietly but do not let yourself be trampled on. I did it by pointing out his handicap to him. After all, is there anyone in this world who can honestly say they are perfect? All of us possess some kind of defect.

There was a member of Brooke Hall (that is, a 'beak' or master) who kept on at me so much that the joke quickly wore off. Every time I opened my mouth to speak to him he mimicked a deaf person and said, 'Pardon' repeatedly. It happened all the time. Even if I was only asking him a simple question like whether the swimming pool was open that afternoon. I never got a reply immediately. He usually carried out this ritual – sometimes for a long time. At first, it was a bit amusing if a bit irritating. As time went on it became plain upsetting. I tried explaining I didn't like it but I was not taken seriously and it continued to a greater extent. I could not simply ignore it as often I had to ask the questions concerned. It got to a point where I was sick and tired of it long before it died away. It was a poor joke. It attacked a point which he knew I could not dispute – that I was deaf. The unfair thing was that as a member of the teaching staff who are on the whole an older and more mature body of people, he should have known when to stop. Furthermore, the fact that he was a beak meant I, as a mere pupil, could not answer back. When I tried once, I was pulled up for it. It was truly 'hitting below the belt'.

These things happen to the best of us, yet it is up to us to make the other person realise his own stupidity without embarrassing him too much. They are the ones who are ignorant of the pain they cause. We are the ones who know and who should put the situation to rights.

As for being the 'Head Man's' daughter, I can't say I suffered at all. Maybe people were more concerned about the fact that I was deaf. Some of the daughters of other more junior beaks had it much worse than I did and were teased unmercifully. Maybe I was not teased for fear of upsetting me because I was also deaf? I think not: even when people did know me well enough to have teased me if they had wanted to, I still never suffered. At least they knew that I could stick up for myself. The majority of the people who were given a rough time tended to be those who couldn't. Some other girls who were overweight or less than attractive, or members of a minority religious group, or below average intelligence were often subjected to mockery. The boys' worst weapon was their merciless observation. Nobody escaped.

Few people made reference to my father. He was a much more remote figure than the immediate beaks whom we saw every day in hash. Once I remember a beak giving us a 'cut' (letting us off the rest of the lesson) because he had a bad headache. As he let us go he said, 'Look you rotten lot – I don't care what you do until the official end of the hash but for God's sake don't walk past the Head Man's study, bang on the window, wave and blow kisses at him. And that goes for you too, Rees!'

Sport became increasingly important to me during my years at Charterhouse and the amount I did was well above average for a *Carthusienne*. It provided me with a means whereby I could rid myself of any frustrations accumulated in the course of the day. A good run after lunch for half an hour or so often released the tension caused by my inability to join in the conversation at the table during the meal. A three mile jog in the morning would wake me up sufficiently to face the day ahead. A game of squash or rackets was a means of relaxation from the constant lipreading as well as a means of socialising on a small scale. I especially enjoyed Rackets. I was the first girl at Charterhouse to take it up on a permanent basis. I also did a lot of swimming with the boys' teams and they all looked after me very well. Once, during very cold weather, Toby, the Captain, made all the other boys remain in the water a while longer freezing to death as they did so while he told me to get dressed in the boy's heated changing room. The age of chivalry is not totally cremated yet.

Trampolining was one of my favourite sports as it was such fun but at the same time jolly hard work. This enabled me to forget everything which was irritating me or getting on top of me. After an hour or so of throwing myself around things never seemed as bad as they had previously appeared.

Sport was important to me therefore, not only physically but socially as well. It provided a means by which I could meet people and communicate with them. This is part of the reason for the *Sport for the Disabled* clubs which exist all over the country. I belong to the Rugby branch. Rugby is one town where facilities for and attitudes towards the disabled are excellent. I go along and meet other disabled people and at the same time I can do something with them, not for them. It is also very good for me to see people far worse off than I am – a constant and effective deterrent to self-pity.

Yet quite apart from all this is the fact that if one is physically fit, one is able to face up to the mental strain of being deaf in a hearing environment far better. Furthermore at the end of the day, if I am physically tired as well as mentally, I sleep more soundly. The next day is then not so difficult as it would be if I had not slept so well. Before I discovered the dividends sport would bring, I slept badly. I went to bed mentally exhausted from lipreading and working, but my body was not tired enough to let me sleep. This all put me under further unnecessary stress which has now largely been eliminated thanks to the discovery of sport.

Another thing I did at Charterhouse was to take up a musical instrument – or rather two. I enjoyed hitting the drums and blowing the clarinet. I did not see why I should be denied it just because of the fact I'm deaf. You may well ask how I could possibly get any pleasure from it if I could not hear it? The answer to that is simple. I couldn't hear it but I got a different sort of pleasure. I could feel the vibrations I made and so I 'knew' what music was. Different vibrations blending together had the effect on me that several notes blending together have upon the ears of hearing people. Hearing people don't seem to realise how important music can be to a deaf individual. There is a misconceived idea that any form of music is denied to the deaf and this wrong opinion is what The Beethoven Fund for Deaf Children run by Ann Rachlin is doing so much to put right. But there is another more subtle point as to why deaf children should be encouraged rather than discouraged as far as music is concerned.

Obviously good speech is an advantage. I have been lucky in that my speech is reasonably intelligible and so I have had few problems making myself understood. This requires constant attention, however, and in this respect music has helped me a great deal. Clarinet and percussion have both helped in different ways. The method of playing the clarinet requires controlled breathing, hence one also learns how to control one's breath while speaking. Since taking up the clarinet my speech has become much more controlled and the breathless squeaks at the end of my sentences, which used to be a frequent occurrence, have now been almost obliterated. The method of stressing certain notes on the drums has helped my intonation, and my voice is far less monotonous than it once was. Indeed monotone voices are very typical of deaf people, and not being able to hear my own voice I am grateful I have avoided that particular pitfall with the help of music. A deaf child can be taught stress by tapping out the rhythm with a pencil. He or she can be taught controlled breathing by other classroom techniques. Yet music is a far more vital and entertaining way of doing it. It is a pleasure to hit the drum and make a noise while also learning something. With the help of music, speech lessons ceased, for me, to be such a bore.

I used to play the drums in the Charterhouse Chapel with the Brass Band during a few certain hymns which always had this accompaniment. I could not see the conductor from where I was standing and so I often relied on someone to give me my cue. I vividly remember this going wrong once and I was accidently given my cue at the wrong moment. Members of the congregation were suddenly startled by a loud crescendo on the drums during some quiet organ music!

Speech can be so vital to a deaf person that anything which can be done to improve it should be considered. The Beethoven Fund for Deaf Children has done much to put music forward as a means of speech therapy and I feel this idea could be extended even further. There are several other similarly surprising sources of therapy. My mother had a 'thing' about poetry. I agree with her. Once I could lipread, read and pronounce words properly, poetry was used to advance my oral education even further.

CHAPTER FIFTEEN

Temporary Employment

Despite the good times I had at Charterhouse, there were bad times as well, and like any other Carthusian I had patches of ups and downs from time to time. The good times were frequent, the bad far and few between. Memories of the good times are those which many other Carthusians share: the warm summer afternoons spent watching cricket on Green or lazing around on Founders Court; the thrill of getting a 'cut' from a lesson when the Master failed to turn up; evening Chapel, traditional during the last week of the summer term where we would sing 'Jerusalem' and 'Turn Back, O Man', to the accompaniment of trumpets and the rest of the brass orchestra.

The bad times affected me to a profound extent. I started off doing French 'A'-level but had to give it up. This was because of the oral, aural, and dictation part of it. As far as the written work and grammar was concerned, I could more than hold my own. But as it was, the examination board which the school liaised with could not make any exceptions for me. Life became increasingly difficult as far as French was concerned. We also had set books for literature which we read out aloud in class and I could not follow well enough to gain much from it. Sometimes the teaching was done in French and that really proved my stumbling block. First, I cannot actually speak French very well. Phonetically I can pronounce the words, but I have no trace of an accent at all. I've never heard one and so can't reproduce it. Secondly, every French work I lipread has to be individually learnt: it is difficult to figure out one word from the rest by the context of the sentence. You either know or you don't, and this limits the number of words one can learn so I didn't know very many. Hence at the end of the summer term in my first year, despite much help from my teachers, I had to give it up. As my French teacher wrote on my report, it was 'in many ways a great pity'. It was impossible. I worked hard at it but even so I had to divide my time evenly between my four subjects if I was to cope. I could not afford to concentrate solely on French.

I got upset when I had to give it up. I felt such a failure and I hated my deafness for it. I always have and always will try not to blame my deafness for anything that goes wrong, but it was clearly to blame as far as French was concerned. If it had not been for the oral side of the subject, I would have managed. The final straw came the following spring, nine months after I had given the subject up. It was announced that my group were taking the examinations under a different board. My frustrations nearly exploded. This different board might have been more willing to make allowances. I felt angry and even ashamed at my handicap. I even felt a sense of guilt that I had not really tried hard enough. I kept wondering what might have been if I had not given it up there and then.

Any failures I suffered were not in any way a reflection on the teaching staff. The intellectual atmosphere was excellent and of a very high standard indeed. What got me down were the inadequacies caused by my handicap which led to a build-up of frustration within me. And although I hesitate to blame my deafness for everything, I felt that it seemed to present me with so many hurdles it was often too much to face getting over them all. Often it was tempting to retreat, to withdraw from my problems and to avoid contact with other people to save the bother of having to lipread them. But I always managed somehow, with the help of close friends, to pull through. They would encourage me when the going got rough and remind me of what I could do rather than point out what I couldn't do. This helped a lot. Moral support is vital for a deaf person. Without it, one feels lacking in self-confidence and tends to dwell on one's bad points rather than emphasize good qualities. I kept telling myself I was comparatively well off. I could speak well, I wasn't stupid, I wasn't ten stone overweight, I didn't have a face like Frankenstein, I was able to have hearing boy friends unlike many of my deaf friends who couldn't cope in hearing environments, I had qualifications, I was comparatively better off than the millions on the dole queue, I could hold an intelligent conversation, I could read, I could write. I was *lucky*. The average reading age of a deaf school leaver is eight. And this declines to five by the time the adult reaches twenty-two years of age. That is a fact. For most sufferers, deafness is cognitive poverty.

In spite of all the difficulties I had to face up to, I still feel that it is a good idea for deaf students to go to a hearing school for the sixth form if they are able to do so. It lessens the deaf person's awe and fear of hearing people and it increases the hearing person's understanding of the handicap. This improves the level and quantity of communication between the two groups.

After a year at Charterhouse my ability to get on with the hearing world had ceased to give me cause for concern. I began to feel as if I was part of 'their group' and not an alienated outsider. I ceased to think of 'them' and 'me'. It was with this in mind that amongst other factors I began to consider the prospect of a university career which I had previously neglected. I felt that it was a possibility now whereas before I'd lacked the confidence to do it.

My mother had been at Oxford as had my grandparents and my aunt. After much thought and discussion I decided to attempt the entrance exam to Balliol College, Oxford.

This was how I found myself sitting in the big Hall at Charterhouse on Monday 23rd November 1981, nervously awaiting the General Paper.

I found the Oxbridge exams hard but feasible. The week after they had finished was one of the most nail-biting weeks I have ever had cause to live through. Almost everybody who takes the exam to Oxford has an interview afterwards when they go up to the University and are seen by the dons. But if the dons decide that your performance in the written examination does not merit an interview, they send you a letter of cancellation and you are rejected. I dreaded such a letter dropping through the letterbox in that week between the exams and the interview. Some of my friends received them and got terribly upset. I shuddered at the thought of it happening to me. 'No news was indeed good news' during that time.

Right up until I left for my interview no such letter had arrived and I began to breathe more freely. I left the house and went to the station to catch the train, where just when I least expected it, disaster struck. It was during the spell of snow in early December 1981 and the trains were either cancelled or faced long delays. It was all thanks to my father, who paid for a taxi, that I got to Oxford in time.

The date of my interview was the third anniversary of my mother's death and as I entered the room I could see her saying, 'Sock it to the old fogies!' with a huge grin on her face. 'Okay then, I will,' I muttered grimly as I entered.

I heard I had been accepted at about 11.30 at night when Dad and the rest of my family burst into my room where I was asleep yelling something about a 'phone call from Balliol. All we had in the house to celebrate with at the time was some disgusting Portuguese sparkling rosé wine. But we drank it anyway.

A lot of praise was due to my teachers from all the years of my life that I had achieved this very great honour. The teachers of Mary Hare and Charterhouse, not to mention those from the primary schools I attended. To me, my acceptance at Balliol was proof that my idea to go to a hearing school had worked. I had coped in a hearing environment and gained a place at University as a result of it. The outcome of my and everyone else's efforts had been highly positive – not negative as I had at one time subconsciously feared.

The Christmas holidays after I got into Oxford were highly entertaining. It was then that I had my first taste of a job and being at work.

Rugby, where we lived now, was an area of high unemployment and finding work was hard for anyone, including myself. After several futile attempts at job hunting, I finally landed a job pulling pints behind the bar in one of Rugby's many pubs. Rumour has it that Rugby has more pubs per square mile than any other town in Britain apart from Douglas on the Isle of Man. I can well believe it. The town is simply festooned with them and the streets are at their busiest at 11.10 on a Friday night.

I had had no previous experience of working behind bars but

I managed to convince the bloke who interviewed me that I was willing to learn. In the course of conversation I referred obliquely to my hearing loss but I did not admit to being as deaf as I really was. I said I had a slight hearing impairment which resulted in my being an expert lipreader. When his face clouded with doubt, I hastily told him that it would mean I would not have any difficulty hearing the orders from customers if the music was too loud, I would simply lipread them instead. This seemed to satisfy him and I walked home elated. I had landed my first job.

Sometimes the availability of employment influences the severity of deafness as a handicap. Deafness imposes conditions upon its victims. A normal response to the social context like finding a job and supporting oneself financially may be impossible for the deaf, not only because of their deafness, but because of restricted opportunities and prejudiced social attitudes. Most deaf people have the ability to acquire employment skills, but they rarely do so. The skills they do develop may be far below the necessary level, or they may be close but not quite adequate. Hence in times of high unemployment, the less able are likely to find it harder to get work and are therefore categorised as being in need of help. This only serves to worsen the feelings of inferiority which often accompany deafness since the person feels more and more inadequate at not being able to support himself.

I am one of the lucky ones. I can speak and communicate with hearing people and therefore sham my way through a great many situations by pretending to be able to hear more than I actually can and hence get jobs more easily. It is no good if the deaf unemployed blame the 'uncaring hearing world' for everything. It is often up to the deaf person to make the initial positive determined effort with the employer. It is no good just simply sitting at home and blaming the rest of the world for the fact that you have not got a job. I vividly remember once having a long conversation with a deaf friend of mine about employment prospects for the deaf. We were both moaning about the types of jobs we could not do. I pointed out that I could not work on the stock exchange or any job requiring a telephone, nor would I be much good as a doctor if I could not hear a cardiac arrest alarm. But in the midst of our conversation a thought suddenly struck me, and it struck me so hard I was temporarily at a loss for words. Okay, we the deaf can't often get the jobs we want because of the fact we can't hear, but millions more people out there can't get the jobs they want because they haven't got the qualifications. Who were we to moan? I might be deaf but I do have qualifications and so I am 'equal' to those who have no qualifications but who can hear. Those who do have qualifications and can also hear are the lucky ones. The people worst off are the handicapped with no qualifications whatsoever. That is a plight which is just to terrible to ignore.

I found after a while that I could manage in the pub provided the customers weren't too drunk. When they did get drunk I found them very difficult to lipread, which meant one of the other girls had to listen for me. On the other side of the coin, the girls could understand what the customers were saying provided the music wasn't too loud. Whenever the music got really loud as the evening went on, the girls were unable to hear the orders and I had to lipread for them. It was all give and take in a most amicable manner. The logical conclusion of all this is that when the music was loud and the customers were drunk we were all hopelessly lost and it was 'every man for himself' in the last hour before closing time when conditions were such.

This led to some embarrassing lipreading mistakes. To make matters worse the bloke in charge was extremely fussy about wasting drinks. He would get really annoyed if you gave the customer the wrong order and wasted any of his precious liquid by doing so. I was always mislipreading orders and annoying the customers by doing so. It was just my bad luck that he usually happened to be standing nearby me whenever I made my mistakes. The final straw happened when a tallish bloke leaned over the counter and beckoned me to serve him. As luck would have it it was late in the evening and the music was loud and the bloke intolerably drunk. I asked him what he wanted and all I got of his order was 'Three haaa . . . arr . . .' I asked him to repeat it 'Three haáa . . . arr . . .' was all I got again. I racked my brains to put two and two together and came up with 'Three half pints lager'. I presumed this was what he wanted and feeling rather pleased with myself I briskly filled the glasses and placed them on the counter in front of him. I was aghast when I realised that the order was wrong. He wanted three Hamlet cigars.

That was the last night I served in that pub. I wasn't exactly given the sack – just told 'not to worry about coming in again' and given a large bonus of money to dissolve any ill feelings. I can't remember really minding. I was trying too hard to keep a straight face all the while. It was only two days before I was due to leave anyhow. Everyone said that at least I'd tried instead of just hiding away at home with only back numbers of the *Reader's Digest* to keep me company. The large bonus certainly came in handy. It was more than I would have earned if I'd worked the two extra days.

Yet I view it all in a positive light. I'd had a taste of real earn-your-living-type work and I'd made several new friends not to mention a generous addition to my store of anecdotes.

After leaving Charterhouse but before going to Oxford, I worked for six weeks at the Sainsburys Store in the Rugby Shopping Centre. I really enjoyed that. The staff were friendly, the atmosphere relaxed and the standards of hygiene were extremely high.

Before I got the job however, I had to attend for an interview with the store's personnel manager. She was exceedingly pleasant and did not seem put out by the fact I was deaf. Rather she seemed impressed by it and regarded it as a point in my favour. One of the first questions she asked me was: 'Being deaf and therefore disabled, what kind of person would be the most likely type to annoy or upset you?' To which I replied: 'Someone who refused to give me a chance to prove myself, but rejected me solely on the grounds that I'm deaf without even considering my good points', and as an afterthought I added, 'Like someone who rejected my application for a job without bothering to give me an interview or even consider me just because my ears don't work.' She grinned – she couldn't have failed to get the hint. The interview lasted just over an hour and at the end of it she told me how interested she'd been to find out more about deafness. Then as she shut her file she told me that there was no reason why she should not employ me. I had done it. I, a deaf person, had got a job with hearing people in spite of the fact I could not hear. They actually wanted me for myself.

My sister Natasha also got a job at the same store and we started work together. We were met and taken upstairs to be given our uniforms and there I nearly lost my job. The girl who was 'breaking us in' spoke too fast and I had to tell her I was deaf. I was surprised, surely she ought to have known since the personnel officer would have made sure of it? When I told her, she looked a bit surprised and went to get the manager who came in saying, 'Jessica, does the Personnel Officer know you are deaf?' 'Of course', I replied, 'I told her everything and she employed me in spite of it.' I was getting annoyed. Natasha didn't know what to do. 'What are you going to do about fire alarms?' he queried. I thought rather sarcastically to myself that I would hardly stand still in the middle of the store with everyone belting for the exit. 'Could you hear a fire alarm?' he asked. I replied that I could feel the vibrations and that I would undoubtedly know that there was one since I was never to be on my own. Satisfied, he let the matter rest and I began my employment there by being shown a series of films on shoplifting, hygiene, customer service and store policy. During the film the girl who was looking after us kept stopping the reel to explain to me what was being said. This was a great help and in general it reflected the attitudes of everyone there. They were all willing to help me whenever I needed help.

After a week, I was transferred to the tills and trained as a cashier. The lady who trained us treated me no differently except to speak more clearly so that I could follow. Surely this is one of the best policies a store can have towards any disabled employees. I was never made to feel a burden and nobody was patronising towards me either.

I wore a badge which said 'Customer: I will lipread what you say' and some customers actually asked me why. When I told them it was because I was deaf some of them thought I was joking and went really red when I revealed that honestly I could not hear. I was subjected to some abuse, but not much. I had one customer who when she heard I was deaf told me Sainsburys had only employed me out of pity and that I shouldn't really be allowed to work in a place where the children could see me. I got visibly upset at this and the customer behind her gave her a right telling off and told her she should be ashamed of herself. Then she turned to me and told me, 'Not to worry luv, it's them people who are stupid'. Most of the people were really pleased and once they heard I was deaf they seemed interested and told me that I was doing well and that they were pleased to have met me.

I was sitting at the till one day and a middle aged woman came through. After ringing up her order I turned to her and said, 'Five pounds, eighty-six pence please'. She gave me a look of bewilderment. I repeated myself but she still didn't seem to understand. I couldn't quite pinpoint what was wrong until she handed me a square piece of cardboard which said: 'I am deaf and I do not speak or lipread very well. Please write down what you wish to say to me. I use the manual sign language alphabet.' I just sat back in my chair and started signing to her cheerfully. She was amazed. Using sign language she told me that Sainsburys had a reputation for stocking the more unusual goods such as mangoes and other foreign delicacies, but she had no idea they also stocked cashiers fully trained in sign language. We conversed for a few minutes at the expense of the other customers waiting in the queue, but nobody seemed to mind. It was all very amusing.

I was sorry to leave Sainsburys when I did. The job was only supposed to last for six weeks but I was told I could come back at Christmas.

•

Oxford and the prospect of studying there for three years for a Zoology degree was looming up. The time for me to start at Balliol College was coming nearer and nearer. I started to get very tense. Would I be able to cope? What if I could not lipread any of my tutors or lecturers? Would I be able to cope with the faster pace of the social life that existed there? Would the people be as open, frank and friendly as had formerly been the case in my education? Would I be able to hold my own against the intellectual élite? What would happen if it all went horribly wrong?

I was determined to make a go of it and during the first week in October, my father and I loaded up the car in the pouring rain and off we went.

CHAPTER SIXTEEN

Spires Without Bells

I made a big mistake when I went up to Oxford, because I arrived too early. It was unavoidable in the circumstances but it meant I was more or less left to my own devices for the first day or so. The official time when the freshers had to arrive was on Wednesday evening in time for the Freshers' Dinner. Most of them arrived during the afternoon beforehand. Hence after I had finished unpacking I had nothing to do except wander round town or read in my room. I quickly became very lonely indeed. I was deaf, in a new place and had nobody I knew whom I could talk to. For the most part I hid in my room drinking endless cups of coffee not knowing quite what to do with myself. I didn't dare go out and say 'Hello' to someone in case I could not lipread them.

By seven o'clock on the first evening I was really feeling pretty low when suddenly there was a loud knock on my door and Wayne came to the rescue. He had been in my House at Charterhouse and was now in the second year at Balliol reading physics and philosophy. I've never been so glad to see anyone in my life. Things immediately began to look up. He took me out into the garden quad where he introduced me to a lot of his friends but there my heart sank again. They all looked so friendly and talked animatedly but I could not lipread a single one of them. I immediately felt uneasy. It was my first taste of the real hearing world, away from home or school, and to my dismay it looked as if it was going to be even more difficult than I had thought. Everybody spoke too fast and turned their heads away so that I could not see all of what they were saying. They waved their arms about distractingly and held their glasses containing their drinks or their cigarettes in front of their faces – both actions which obscured their lips and made it even more difficult for me to lipread. Few of them enunciated clearly, it was all in mumbled words and phrases. I found it very difficult to understand, and I found myself becoming an acutely self-conscious observer, a frustrated onlooker. I began to hate my deafness which was preventing me from participating. None of them were malicious or intentionally neglectful by any means, they all smiled at me when introduced and said 'Hello'. It was just that they were more keen to talk to their old established friends whom they had not seen since June. Some of them were not aware I was deaf and if they were, they probably did not realise how difficult I was finding it to follow. But it did make me feel even more lonely and cut off. I was truly isolated in a crowd and if it had not been for Wayne I would probably have run back to my room to hide there and then.

We went into the college bar known as the 'Buttery' where we were found by even more people. At one point there were fifteen of us standing round in a circle with conversation flowing freely. I was unable to detect what they were talking about, I could not keep pace with the verbal output as it darted swiftly from lip to lip. I became more and more fed up.

A small group of us then went to a pub for supper where the lighting was bad which worsened the situation even further. Now I could not even see to lipread people when they spoke to me alone. I felt tired and all I wanted to do was go to bed. I persevered however, and things did get better later on when we went back to Wayne's room for coffee and group lessened to about three in number. Lipreading immediately became easier, I relaxed and I laughed more. They began to speak to me in a clearer way so that I could understand them better. Most of them were interested in the fact I was deaf. I represented a novelty to them, for few had actually come to face to face with a person of my handicap before. I was bombarded with questions about lipreading, sign language and differing degrees of deafness. Since I was at home in these subjects, I regained confidence bit by bit and began talking back to them more and more. By the time I finally got to bed, things were much better.

One advantage of having been at Charterhouse was that Oxford was full of Carthusians, many of whom I knew or recognised from my days at school there. If I had come to Oxford straight from the Mary Hare, I would have only known one girl in Somerville who had been in the year above me at that school. As it was, I had several people whom I knew and whom I could go around with at first. Life might have been much more difficult otherwise.

I sat next to the Master at the Freshers' Dinner the following night and as I walked in, I realised with an awful feeling that the lighting was hardly sufficient to lipread by. Fortunately it was better up by High Table and I did not have too many problems. Grace was said, it consisted solely of two Latin words and was over very quickly. As we sat down, the Master said to me in low tones, 'You can see we've got the shortest grace possible!' I found it very amusing. After dinner he gave a speech welcoming all the Freshers to Balliol and it was the first speech I have ever been able to lipread in its entirety. This was obviously due to the fact I was sitting right next to him but it came to me as a startling thought that it was the only time in all of my nineteen years I had managed to follow every single word. Formerly the announcement of a speech had meant that I had to amuse myself for fifteen minutes or so as the speaker droned on and on. I would write notes or sign to my neighbours or just look around at everyone else. I had never been close enough to lipread the whole thing before and this came as a pleasant surprise.

I was brought back down to earth with a bump in the Junior Common Room after the dinner however, as I could not lipread the speeches there given by various members of the JCR Committee. There was free drink which probably explained it. People are very difficult to lipread when they are drunk. But I find it even more difficult to lipread when I am the one that is drunk! I decided it was a combination of the two factors which caused this temporary inability.

I quickly became able to lipread the people whom I had found difficult at first. One of my friends, Cameron, was not slow to realise that I relied a lot on the context of the sentence to be able to understand certain words. As I've said before, lipreading could almost be called mindreading since only 30% of speech sounds are lipreadable. In a sentence of ten words, I pick up about four and place the rest together, e.g. If I picked up 'going, shopping, shoes' together with a few odd consonants, it would most likely mean, 'I'm going to go shopping to buy a new pair of shoes.' Similarly I rely on clues given by the context of the conversation to help me. If somebody starts talking about the space shuttle, it immediately eliminates irrelevant vocabulary and astronautical terms are those that come to mind whilst reading somebody's lips. If somebody were to make a remark about John Donne in the middle of a conversation about the space shuttle, the chances are that I would not get it. They would have to make it clear they were talking about poetry first. Cameron took great advantage of this and went out of his way to infuriate me by introducing and inserting facetious remarks into his sentences when he spoke to me to try and throw me out. He would suddenly say things like 'Little pink monkeys' or 'Banana yoghurt' while talking about something completely different and roar with sadistic laughter at my bewilderment. I spent a lot of time resolving to get my own back.

I managed it one day about two or three months later during a train journey between Reading and Oxford in a high speed train. Marc, Cameron, Penny and I were coming back from a party at Marc's house complete with hangovers and headaches. Three of us were sitting on one side of the aisle while Cameron was seated opposite a very pompous looking gentleman on the other. Cameron began mouthing abstract rude remarks about the other people in the carriage to me which neither Penny nor Marc could lipread. We held this silent conversation for a while until Marc got exasperated and asked me what Cameron was saying so I repeated Cameron's most recent remark. Only I did not realise how loud my voice was so not only did Marc and Penny hear, but so did other people who were not supposed to. There was a stunned silence and then Cameron went bright red as he realised the man opposite him must have heard the very rude comment he had made about him, which was probably untrue to boot. The rest of us nearly split our sides. Revenge was indeed sweet. Cameron had to continue sitting opposite this man for a further fifteen minutes in an awkward silence before we finally reached Oxford.

I can usually control the level of my voice. But in a quiet environment, like most deaf people, because I do not realise how very quiet it is, I don't notice how over-loud my voice sounds when I talk in what I feel to be normal tones. That is to say I do not always appreciate the need to lower my voice. This can lead to some embarrassing moments. I remember once my mother telling me to be quiet in Notre Dame in Paris because I informed her in my normal voice (which of course echoed loudly throughout the hushed atmosphere of the cathedral) that a lady who was praying was wearing a revolting bright pink hat. Likewise when I am told something about somebody nearby, I cannot always tell that the speaker has lowered his voice. So I reply in ringing tones instead of whispers which makes my interlocutor cringe and the person under discussion indignant. This often happens and the general course of the incident goes:

Wayne (very quietly): 'Look at John's jumper.'

Me (in normal tones and looking at John as I do so): 'Why, what's wrong with John's jumper?'

Wayne: 'Shhhh!'

Me: 'Oh sorry.'

John: 'Hey you – what are you being rude about me for?' Wayne now has to apologise and is very embarrassed.

Once while waiting at Charing Cross station with Wayne and Henri for our train to Paris, I was reading a book to pass the time. It was a book of amazing facts and stated very explicitly that Henry VIII had had the largest codpiece which was now in the Tower of London. I wasn't quite sure what a codpiece was. If anything, I would guess it to be a large piece of fish. I had never heard of one and since my vocabulary was not as extensive as that of my hearing contemporaries, I decided to ask Wayne. He was just walking away as I decided to so hence I shouted at him in loud tones and I'm sure everyone within fifty square metres heard.

'Wayne, what is a codpiece?'

He spun round looking slightly shocked and already going red, 'Jessica! For God's sake will you shut up, it's rude!' I thought he was only joking so I persisted and continued to ask him what it was, only this time in quieter tones. But he was too embarrassed by the previous happening and held up a newspaper between us pretending not to know me.

I was not the only disabled student at Balliol. Wayne had an artificial left leg caused by cancer when he was sixteen. We often used to compare our disabilities. His put a limit to his mobility but it did not interfere with his study. Mine made lectures very difficult and hence interfered with my work but it did not limit my mobility. It was difficult to decide which was worse; each felt the other was worse off. We had a common alliance and it was quite useful sometimes. There was one occasion when somebody was teasing me by speaking to me but putting his hand in front of his mouth so that I could not lipread. Wayne suddenly nudged my arm and said very pointedly, 'Don't worry Jessica, it's normal people again, they're just so odd' and turned the tables on the other guy who immediately blushed.

I was seldom conscious of Wayne's artificial leg. I always forgot about it since it was so rarely visible. This led to some rather painful moments when he insulted me and I retaliated by kicking him and ended up clutching my toe in agony. He often forgot I was deaf and spoke to me from behind. Once at a party when the music was loud I happened to ask him to repeat something he had said. The reason I had been unable to lipread had been bad lighting but he naturally assumed it was due to the loudness of the music. Before either of us realised anything he had cupped his hands over his mouth and had moved closer to my ear. By the time we had stopped laughing, he had forgotten what it was he had been going to say.

Handicaps can sometimes be invisible even to the handicapped themselves. I went along one afternoon to talk to the Physiology Tutor at Holywell Manor who asked me why I found lectures difficult to follow. I told him precisely why and said that it was often difficult for hearing people to appreciate the problems deaf people have. He listened patiently and then just before I rose to go, he asked me if he could tell me something. Of course I said yes, but I was completely taken aback when he announced with a quiet smile that he too was deaf, and showed me his hearing aid to prove it. I felt at a loss for words for quite a while afterwards.

Another amusing incident had occurred with a blind friend of mine. Anne and I were walking around the Charterhouse grounds arm in arm in the summer of 1979. It was a hot sunny day and we chattered away perfectly normally about everything and nothing. I guided her movements and she told me when there was a car coming, it was truly a symbiotic relationship with both sides benefiting mutually. Suddenly as we were half-way across a field there was a sudden flash of lightning accompanied by a loud cracking noise. 'Look!' I shouted to her 'Listen!' she shouted to me. It was a few moments before the sickening irony sank in. Sometimes when two or more handicapped people are together, the handicaps cancel each other out and you forget them. It is certainly true that I was more aware of my deafness whilst at Charterhouse than I was whilst at Mary Hare. At the latter place, you tended to forget about deafness after a while simply because everyone was deaf. Hence being deaf was the norm, it was not so unusual as to be a major topic for conversation. You simply forgot consciously to acknowledge its existence.

The people at Balliol were quick to adjust to my hearing loss. Even the porters in the lodge adapted. Whenever I was away and wanted to give a message to somebody in college I knew I could ring the lodge and dictate it over the 'phone. It was quite simple. They could not talk to me, and did not complicate matters by trying to either, but I could at least get across what I wanted to say while they took it down. I always repeated it twice, but there was no way they could check by asking me. They co-operated marvellously over this and it certainly made life much easier for me as it meant I could do it myself instead of having to cause a lot of trouble and nuisance and get someone else to do it for me all the time. In fact all the college staff were helpful right from the Domestic Bursar who made arrangements for me to have a visual fire alarm put into my room, all the way down to the Buttery staff who cheerfully kept me topped up.

The staff at the college treated me as they would any other normal student and in doing so paid me one of the highest compliments possible. I was given a room three floors up a winding staircase in the front quad – crazy, you might say, because of the risk of fire and my not hearing the alarm in time, but in fact I was in a sense flattered that it had not occurred to them to treat me any differently. Later they offered to move me down if I so wished and this only elevated my opinion of them. Right from the start I was given the opportunity to be a normal student and was not fussed over because of my handicap.

The academic side of university life did not run quite so smoothly however, and it was in this area that I really became unstuck and unable to cope. I am aware that I was not the only handicapped student at Oxford, indeed there were many others: thalidomide victims, blind or those with limited mobility to name but a few besides myself. But their problems were different from mine. Those with limited mobility had problems getting to lectures etc., but once they were there they were at least able to understand what was being said. I'm not saying they were any better off than I was, just that they were in a different category altogether and, selfish though it may seem, it is the problems which I had that I will deal with here. But before I begin I would like to point out a few facts.

Of all the sensory and physical handicaps, deafness is educationally the most serious because it can initially impair the child's ability to acquire normal language; one wages a constant war against cognitive poverty. It is one of the least well understood by the hearing public. It is not an overt problem like blindness or physical handicap and is hence often misinterpreted or even worse, ignored in institutions of higher education but I hope that what I am saying will light up corners in dark rooms and illuminate the problems which deaf students often come across at this level of learning. I am not so much concerned here with the primary and secondary education of the deaf student, critical as they are. I am assuming that by reaching higher education, the deaf student has largely overcome the linguistic handicap. But again this depends on several factors, the character and intelligence of the student and the amount, if any, of useful residual hearing he has, not to mention the background and the quality of education received. But even if the child is intelligent, outgoing and comes from a stable background it does not necessarily mean that his university career will be problem-free. Indeed mine certainly wasn't.

CHAPTER SEVENTEEN

University Challenge

As I outlined briefly in the previous chapter, my most immediate problem was being unable to follow what was said at lectures and seminars. Think of a deaf student sitting through an average of three hours a day, five days a week, of lectures with little if any means of following what the lecturer is saying. The capabilities of lipreading alone are limited. Not only that, it is so tiring that it often only took twenty minutes of desperately trying to grasp the gist of what the lecturer was saying and to make sense of all the diagrams scrawled all over the board to wear me out. I cannot say too many times how difficult lipreading can be, even for those deaf peole with good grasp of language, for many of the sounds of speech are not accompanied by movements of the mouth and lips while for other sounds, the movements are the same. Moreover, lipreading my lectures required a knowledge of the zöological terms, many of which I had never heard of before. Hence I only had access to these new words by the written word. Often the lecturer did not even write the word down, thus denying me any form of verbal access whatsoever. Apart from this I had obvious problems if I could not see the lecturer properly.

I do not blame a lecturer if he does not like looking at his students, many of whom display blatant lack of interest. But I found it so frustrating when the lecturer walked up and down, looked at the floor, spoke to the board as if it were an intimate friend, or looked down at his notes mid-sentence leaving me not knowing which way a statement had gone. Hearing students take these things for granted. In my case I felt an acute sense of failure. I had always been told my lipreading was good. Why then could I not lipread now? Was it my fault?

My first few attempts at following lectures ended up with tears of frustration, impotent rage and feelings of utter despair. The lectures were important to my course. It required far less effort to go to a lecture than to research all the notes oneself in the Radcliffe Science Library.

I was sometimes given lecture notes as a sort of partial answer to the problem of information input but that meant I spent all my spare time frantically copying notes, often well into the small hours, in a bid to keep up. Fellow-students lent me their notes but more often than not they gave me no more than a sketchy outline of the subject with a few oblique references to detail. Also, the average student's interpretation of the lectures was not always correct. This led to even more confusion on my part trying to put it all right again. Some lecturers' notes helped, but these tended to be brief except for one or two who wrote theirs out fully. It was on the whole inadequate and I felt a dismal failure despite having a sympathetic tutor who understood the problem and went miles out of his way to help and encourage me. I simply could not cope.

After a while, finding the lectures such a trial, I simply stopped attending them. This had the immediate effect of isolating me from the other students on my course which meant I had no one apart from my tutors with whom I could discuss the course. I fell more and more behind and partly because of this and partly because I was so isolated from my fellow-students, I began to have difficulty in retaining my enthusiasm for the course. I began to feel I was mad to have ever thought I would be able to cope at a university.

After a brief lapse, following a viral infection which landed me in hospital for six days, I resumed the course with renewed aggression and determination. By now I had three or four one-to-one tutorials per week. To begin with, this was fine, but as time went on it was evident that this was no answer either. I was still isolated, and my collection of vital information still fell a long way short of that of my fellow-students who attented lectures and wrote down in an hour what took me four times as long to get from books. On top of all this extra work to keep up my notes, I now had to prepare three or four tutorial essays a week while the other students only had one or two. Each one required several hours work if it was worth doing at all and I began to run out of time. Inadequately or shoddily done essays were clearly no answer, but what with practicals as well it was simply too much for me to handle. I became more and more frustrated and although I did not admit it to anyone, my feelings of failure were intensified greatly and I was more than ready for the end of my first term when it finally came.

This is not to say that I hated Oxford. Far from it. I loved the city, the people, the atmosphere and the whole essence of university life. The college staff and the dons were friendly. I even liked the work at times and provided my essays were ready I looked forward to the tutorials and to discussing zoological topics with my tutors. It was just rather a strain not being able to keep up as well as I had hoped but this did not spill over into my social life which was completely separate from my work. I had plenty of friends whom I could always go and talk to and with whom I could go out in the evenings. For the most part my friends were 'normal' students, but this was not out of pure choice, rather pure chance as the ratio of disabled students to normal students was so low. I joined in 'normal' pastimes. I played squash, swam, went to films, discos, restaurants and everything that they did. I attended fewer plays but this was understandable because of the lipreading involved and the difficulty of obtaining copies of the script beforehand.

One of the real tests was a debate I attended at the Oxford Union. I was taken by a medical student in Balliol who later became President and who had held my hand during the lumbar puncture I was given in October during the viral infection. To this day he maintains that in my agony I bit his hand during the process. I still refuse to acknowledge it.

We went for dinner beforehand where I was introduced to another deaf lady and seats were reserved for both of us at the front of the house facing the speakers. I managed to follow most of the debate and enjoyed it even though I did not stay for the whole thing. It lasted nearly three hours and I kept up for just two hours before I began to get tired of lipreading. At this point, the Union Bursar rescued me and took me off to the bar for a much needed drink.

But in spite of the good times I had socially, I found being a deaf student at university difficult as far as a scientific course like mine was concerned. There is not much existing provision for the deaf within the framework of higher education. The question one may ask is, 'What do I think should be done judging from my own experiences?' This is difficult. If I were a wheelchair student, the answer would be more clear-cut and would include requests to make buildings and lecture rooms more accessible by building ramps and installing lifts. As it stands, deafness is a difficult problem to solve as far as university life is concerned.

I feel an individual student-need approach would be more useful than just trying to accommodate all deaf students within the existing framework and rigidly give them all the same kind of help. There are, to my mind, two basic types of deaf students in higher education:

(a) deaf students who can integrate into a 'hearing' course with or without support or help. This type of deaf student may be only partially hearing instead of profoundly deaf. There may have a lot of useful residual hearing and be able to cope with lectures with or without the help of acoustic equipment. There should be few linguistic or communication problems for this type of student;

(b) deaf students who because of linguistic impairment or inadequate communication skills are unable to integrate fully on their own into a hearing course. They need a lot of support, but provided it is given they possess the ability to do examination work or vocational courses to a high standard. This group is more likely to include the deafer students.

But the two groups are not always as clear-cut as that. There is no stereotype deaf student. I could list myself as belonging to the first group because I have few communication or linguistic problems and have coped in a hearing school for two years. On the other hand I am deaf enough to belong to the second group and I am unable to exist academically without a lot of support. I fall almost exactly between the two groups.

There are several categories of support which can and should be given to those students who have managed to get as far as university. It is not easy for anyone to reach this educational level and it is doubly difficult for deaf students who have to face far more hurdles and greater odds in order to succeed. They should therefore be given a fair chance at university and receive more help if necessary in order that they may succeed. It is such a waste for them to get this far and then have to give up through no fault of their own. Some of the categories of support which I mention are in effect 'double staffing' and as such represent an additional cost to the college/L.E.A. concerned. But a given student may not require all the types of support listed below. It is a matter of it being there if necessary so that the L.E.A or college may be called on to provide it if it is to meet the needs of all its deaf students. Flexibility is also essential as an individual's needs may change or need to be re-assessed from time to time. If such levels of support were to be firmly established they would provide immense encouragement and assurance to the deaf students, who would then be able to tackle their courses with more confidence. The numbers of deaf students at this level of education would go up. At present many of the deaf shy away from university thus wasting real potential. Balliol College gave me as much help as they could, but they had no readily available guidelines. Everything was done by trial and error. Teachers of the deaf should be readily available to the deaf student for a fixed number of hours per week for language communication, counselling and general guidance. A deaf student may need someone who is a professional and will understand only too well the problems involved (both physical and social). There is a useful role for a last level of support from lecturers who are not fully trained teachers of the deaf but who are willing to spare the time and trouble over a deaf student. They may need to learn sign language and will have to have some idea of the complex psychological problems involved with the deaf.

In cases where the difficulty is communication rather than language, where the deaf student is unable to speak or has unintelligible speech and converses by sign language, an interpreter may be needed. In such cases as mine where lecture notes are crucial, a note-taker would be of immeasurable value. If I could only choose one means of support from those already listed, it would be a note-taker for my lectures. This would have been pretty much the answer to some of the problems I had.

Indirect support from the teacher of the deaf is also vital. It may be very time-consuming, but it is extremely important that the teachers of the deaf should spend time supporting the various lecturers who will have the deaf student in their group. After all how can the lecturers help the deaf student if they themselves have no guidance? I found this a big problem. Some of my lecturers simply had no idea what to do with me even if they were willing to help. There was a notice on their desks which asked them not to walk about and to face the audience whilst speaking but this was not really enough for them to go on. Some tried to slow down so that I could follow better and ended up behind time which meant they then had to rush the last few minutes. This caused the other students to lose out on having facts properly explained to them. Some tried to stand still but as they were unused to it they felt self-conscious and they found themselves lecturing badly and were forced back into their former habits of walking around. Some read aloud from notes and hence had to look down all the time to see what they were reading even if it meant I could not see their lips to follow. Some used the blackboard a lot and so had to face it most of the time. A few simply forgot and some simply couldn't be bothered. Others were of a great help. My genetics tutor gave me a complete set of his lecture notes in full whilst the Head of the Faculty lent me his file to photocopy and offered to give me a few unofficial tutorials if necessary. Others lent me books, gave me reading lists, etc., and my official tutors gave me whatever help they could. The problem was that we had to come to a level of mutual understanding before all this happened. We had to find out exactly what type of help I needed, and in doing so we wasted a lot of time. It was well into the sixth week of the eight-week term before things really started happening by which time I was falling rapidly behind my fellow students. The other problem was that the scope of the course was so broad that it was impossible for me to cover it all adequately. My biochemistry was fine as I had good notes, a good tutor and constant help. In genetics I had good lecture notes, a good tutor who took a lot of trouble, but we did not have enough time to cover all the topics in the tutorials which other students had explained to them in lectures. In biophysics I had no notes, no tutorials and had to pore over books in the Radcliffe Science Library for hours trying in vain to sieve out information and teach myself. In organisms and evolution I had an excellent tutor but no notes. As far as cell biology was concerned I had nothing, full stop. Not even a reading list. Furthermore there were several other zoological topics I had to cover not mentioned here. In short I had too much on my plate. As university life went by I felt I had been forced by my deafness to bite off more than was ever possible to chew. A lot of this could perhaps have been avoided if the people who had dealings with me had had more guidance from professionals. There is no doubt about it, deaf students at Oxford are exceedingly rare. Hence lecturers etc. are bound to have had limited experience of them. This is where indirect support from teachers of the deaf would be of great value. However, this needs to begin prior to the student joining the course and it represents an ongoing commitment which must be allowed for, financially, when considering the overall level of provision to be made for that deaf student.

There are also other means of support which need not represent an extra charge to the L.E.A and should also be considered. These include help from social workers for the deaf where the problems warrant the involvement of those who have a statutory obligation concerning the welfare of deaf people. Support from other deaf adults should also be given. The low self-image of many young deaf adults can, in certain circumstances, be helped by the involvement of a 'successful' deaf adult which will provide a model so often absent in the experience of deaf people. There is also much special equipment on the market such as radio-aids, looped and acoustically treated rooms, access to information technology such as videos and computers. This can all form an important part of the overall support provision.

There is another type of help which can be given to disabled students which many fail to think of. That is help from one's G.P. Mine gave me a lot of help and advice during my time at Oxford. He took an interest in my life and was always willing to discuss any problems I had and boosted my confidence whenever I felt I was losing the fight.

This help proved invaluable, and on many occasions it pulled me through some very sticky patches indeed. I was lucky for my doctor had the time and the patience. Not all deaf students will be as fortunate as I was. Yet I feel support of this type if it is available can be extremely helpful as one feels one always has someone to whom he can talk outside the educational institution. This does not only go for deaf students. Those with other difficulties or emotional problems would also find this type of help reassuring. On the other hand, one must remember that a G.P. is a busy man and one should never take this type of help for granted or call him out unnecessarily.

The most important factor, however, is that the means of communication in providing support services or in special groups should be determined by the wishes and needs of the students involved, as expressed by them. A variety of methods should be available and flexibility should be the keyword of the project. The starting post should be the acceptance of, and respect for, the deaf student as a young pupil.

Balliol were extremely good about it and put themselves out a great deal to help me. But I felt that, if we had arranged affairs properly before the beginning of my time there, many of the problems I had could have been avoided right from the start. A lot of it was the fault of my inability to explain the problem clearly and ask for specific types of help. It was all new ground to both the college and me. Neither of us quite knew exactly what to do at first – meanwhile my frustrations were piling up.

The difficulties built up to such an extent that eventually it was decided I should make a fresh start in October 1983 by which time the problems would have been looked into and the means of helping me sorted out properly. This seemed the most sensible thing to do and the most satisfying answer to the problem for all concerned. Any sense of failure I might have felt was diminished by the prospect of success should I try again. And I don't think my mother would have approved if I gave up altogether. She would have supported me throughout it all.

This is as far as I have got in my life, and as much as I've got to say by way of a message. One important thing I feel is that if the deaf don't succeed they should try again and keep trying. When I try again at Balliol in the autumn I'll make jolly-well sure the same thing doesn't happen again. Furthermore I'll ensure that any future deaf students who come to the university and find it difficult will be able to draw on my experiences. More generally, when future generations of deaf children re-tread my path to adulthood, I hope my story will help to guide them and the educationists whose job it will be to help them.